Common Sense is NOT so Common!

by Webster Henry

Common Sense is NOT so Common

Webster Henry

Copyright © 2013 by Webster Henry

All rights reserved. No part of this publication may be reproduced or transmitted in any form or by any means, electronic or mechanical, including photocopying, recording or by any information storage and retrieval system, without prior permission from the publisher.

Publisher: Webster Henry, websterhenry@outlook.com

First edition — December, 2013

Second edition – May, 2014

ISBN-10: 0988762412

ISBN-13: 978-0-9887624-1-1

Dedication

To all His children:

May God's Light of Love and Peace be with you and your family, our nation, and the world!

Acknowledgements

I would like to thank the following people for their help, input, and support in the development of this book. Much love and blessings to you all!

Stephanie Dinkel, Colin Flood, Lola Hanley, Bill Henry, Matthew Henry, Michael Henry, Kathleen Jonick, Leslie Kelly, Sue Kelly, Barry Morris, Philip Rastocny, and Ted Webster.

I would also like to pay a very special tribute to my mother, Beatrice. She taught me, through her behavior how to support others. I learned that support comes in many different ways!

Prologue

The number one person in my life is Jesus Christ. Christ came into my life when in pain and sorrow I called out to Him, "Lord Jesus Christ help me, I am the walking dead!" There was a knock on my door and a friend signed me up to a seminar and my life slowly began to change. I began to study scripture and "The Word" came alive to me. I began to understand why building a strong foundation of principles is important. I learned how cause and effect lead to consequences. I also learned the difference between knowledge and wisdom, and living a life with God's principles.

I am a sinner. There is forgiveness from our Heavenly Father by believing and having faith in Jesus Christ. He is there for us. Get to know more of the character of Christ and His compassion for others. He moves from within changing lives through changing hearts. Praise to you Lord and Savior.

You will see true value through "God's Word" and the tools that will expand your perception to the good. Our Father will provide insights. Begin with faith in Christ and forgiving yourself and others. With the help of the Holy Spirit, His Spirit will begin to move within your heart. Begin to see the great abundance of God's treasures awaiting you.

Contents

Common Sense is NOT so Common

Why I wrote this book?

NIV Bible Concordance: Forgiveness

NIV Bible Concordance: Greed and Guilt

NIV Bible Concordance: Love

My Story: Believing….Faith & Prayer..God has interceded!

Dig Deep (picture)

Digging Deeper for True Meaning…. Deep Exploration

Before Digging

You are the Clay in the Potter's Hand!

Listen

Questions to Ponder and Answer before Journaling

Foundation Building (picture)

Foundation

Foundation of the Earth

Foundation…Basis…Support

Is God #1 in Your Life?

"Written in Stone"

Blessed are They That Keep His Precepts!

Know…..by the Fruits They Produce!

'…neither can a corrupt tree bring fourth good fruit" Matthew 7:18

Inner Man/Woman

The Hunter vs. the Farmer

Do You Think We Should Judge a Book by its Cover?

Interior Man/Woman

The Human Heart

Grace

Connecting the Dots.......

Peace of Conscience

Truth

Truth…. Justice…… Faith

Believing and Having Faith in God!

…Resolution…Obscurity…Victory….

Four (4) Sides to Man/Woman

Spiritual Side of Man/Woman

Light vs. Darkness

Darkness

After their own Lusts and far away from Sound Doctrine

A Foundation that Leads to Wisdom

Discernment and Wisdom

Secrets to Wisdom

Wisdom and Understanding

Input--------→ Output

Make God the Cause

Effect

The Bible

Common Sense is Not So Common!

They only know what they see!

Bondage

The Yoke of Bondage

..."how great is that darkness!"

Men/Women Love Darkness

From Babe to Maturity

He sets us free!

God Molds Strong Character Traits!

Renewal of Friendship....New Creation in Christ Jesus

Warning....Thoughts have Power!

Wolf in Sheep Clothing (picture)

Woes to Those Who are Wise in Their Own Eyes and Clever in Their Own Sight!

Different Behavior—Personality Types

Aggressive Behavior....Passive-Aggressive Behavior

Continued: Passive-Aggressive Behavior

Assertive Behavior

Controllers

What Fuels Your Engine???

A Fool's Voice

A Heart for God: He Will Awaken Your True and Hidden Self

The Nature of God & God's Nature

The Gospel, the Good News!

Un-forgiveness

Glory to God!

++Jesus ++ Son of God++

++++Jesus++++

Jesus Loves You!

Learn History……His Story

Renewal

"The Holy Bible"

The Great Textbook "The Holy Bible"

Cliffhangers

Part 2 of Cliffhangers

Part 3 of Cliffhangers

Challenges

Part 2 of Challenges

Part 3 of Challenges

Questions to Ponder and Answer for Your Journal

Final

Part 2 of Final

Part 3 of Final

Bottom Line

Part 2 of Bottom Line

Part 3 of Bottom Line

Special Resources

Part 2 of Special Resources

Works Cited (Books and CD ROM)

Work Cited (Internet)

Common Sense is NOT so Common

In order to grasp the essence of why "Common Sense is NOT so Common," I suggest starting from the beginning of the book and not skip around; furthermore, do not judge on sentence structure, dangling participles, and rid of any other distractions, then will you reach the heart of the matter. There are forces that want to keep us in the dark, ignorant, and dependent. Learn about those forces.

My comments are written in Pristina font

All others are written in Times Forum font.

Happy discovery!

Why I Wrote This Book

This is my testimony: Growing up in the 60's, through the Vietnam War, drugs, sex, divorce, and four people I have known were murdered. The country was so divided……..groups of people against the war, poor treatment of returning soldiers, rebellious groups against authority, against the establishment etc. It was time of great division. I had many questions, but no one to answer them. There were things that did not make sense. I was on a quest for years searching for the meaning of life. At one time I thought that I was an atheist because where was God?

Thirty years ago, on my first visit to Tampa, Florida, there was a billboard that read "Common sense is not so common," …I wonder why? So over the years, in conversation, I would say "that does not make sense" and again the words on the billboard came to mind. Ten years later a tragic incident happened in my life. I was so numb that I did not know to cry, was I happy, was I sad? I was frozen. There was a void that I tried to fill, I was stuck, and I called out to Jesus "Jesus, help me, I am the walking dead!" There was a knock on the door and my neighbor invited me to a seminar. That void was filled when the Lord brought me to scripture. The study was not just stories anymore, but took on true meaning once I wholeheartedly put myself into focusing on learning. I began to study in a new way than when I was young. I began to break down scripture verses and scripture began to speak to me personally. The Bible has helped me daily and I thank God everyday for the lessons that He puts on my heart. He has filled that void in many wonderful ways with His saving Graces and Blessings. He gives me that light every day. And every day I grow stronger with His Word!

I will be using the following resources:

- ❖ I will be quoting scripture verses from the following Bibles:
    - o King James Version (KJV)
    - o New International Version (NIV) Life Application Bible with <u>concordance</u> index
    - o New American Standard Bible (NASB)

- ❖ Webster's American Dictionary of the English Language, 1828 Edition

<u>Bible Concordance</u>

The next three pages consist of examples of citations from <u>NIV Bible concordance</u>. The list contains Biblical words and the place to find them in the Bible.

NIV Bible Concordance: <u>Forgiveness</u>

**Note: Scripture verses in red have the words of Jesus

- As demonstrated by Joseph…Genesis 45:17-20 + Genesis 50:15-21
- Understanding God's forgiveness should make us more willing to forgive Genesis 50:15-21 + Romans 12:17-21

- Brings freedom and dignity………………..Leviticus 26:13
- Only anecdote for revenge…………………Judges 15:1f (footnote)
- Doesn't eliminate sin's consequences……...2 Samuel 12:14
- Confession and repentance essential to…….1 Chronicles 21:8
- Demonstrates strength not weakness……….1 Kings 1:52:53
- Conditions for……………………………..2 Chronicles 7:14
- No sin to great for God to forgive………….2 Chronicles 33:12-13   Psalm 51:1-7   Acts 2:14…1 John 2:2f

- Means forgetting the wrong committed against you…Psalm 103:12
- God won't forgive those who don't forgive others….Matthew 6:14-15
- Found only through faith in Christ…John 20:23
- How often should we grant it…..Matthew 18:22
- Don't withhold it from others…..Matthew 18:35
- Admitting the need for………….Mark 1:5
- Love should be the response to Jesus forgiveness…Luke 7:47
- Use it first before judging others…..John 8:7
- Must lead to a change of heart……. John 8:11
- How it is tied to obedience………….John 8:51
- The key to our relationship with God....Luke 11:4
- Why sin against the Holy Spirit is unforgivable….Luke 12:10
- Don't resent God's forgiveness of others…Luke 15:32
- Jesus forgave His disciples…..Mathew28:10
- Jesus forgives His murderers….Luke 23:34
- Only way to God's power……Acts 8:18-23
- How to experience the joy of…..Romans 4:6-8
- Christ exchanges His forgiveness for our sin….Roman 4:25
- Why we should forgive our enemies…Romans 12:19-21
- God wants to forgive us…….1 John 1:9

NOTES

NIV Bible Concordance: <u>Greed and Guilt</u>

Greed

- Can lead us to sinful surroundings….Genesis 14:12
- Lust leads to …..Numbers 11:34
- Of Korah………Numbers 16:1-3
- Often disguised as ambition…..Numbers 16:8-10
- Blinds us to God's guidance…..Numbers 22:20-23…Deuteronomy 6:10-13
- Can cause you to lose everything…2 Chronicles 10:16-19
- Following God only for what you can get…Jeremiah 37:2-3
- Caused Judas to betray Jesus…..Matthew 26:14-15
- Comes from pride……James 4:4-6
- Using religion for personal enhancement….2 Peter 2:15

Guilt

- Involving others to ours…..Genesis 3:6-7
- Warns us of wrong doing….Genesis 3:7-8
- Joseph's brothers tried to avoid…..Genesis 37:26-27
- Admitting guilt is only part of the true repentance…Numbers 14:40-44
- Be careful of accusing others of….Numbers 35:11-28
- Comes from trying to fulfill rash vows….Judges 11:34:35
- Don't let guilt keep you from praying…Judges 16:28-30
- Shouldn't cripple believers…..Psalm 19:12-13
- Absence of guilty conscience doesn't mean you're doing right..Jonah 1:4-5
- Pilate couldn't wash his away…..Matthew 27:24f
- Of religious leaders for Jesus' death…..John 19:11
- Why all are guilty before God….Roman 2:17ff
- How to be declared "not guilty" before God…..Romans 3:21-29
- Why we are guilty for Adam's sin….Romans 5:12
- How to forget past guilt…..Philippians 3:13-14…1 Timothy 1:12-17

NOTES

NIV Bible Concordance: <u>Love</u>

- Loving those who wrong us……Matthew 5:38-42
- What it means to love your enemies…Matthew 5:43-44
- Talking about it vs. demonstrating it…..Matthew 9:5-6
- Nothing can take God's love from us…..Matthew 10:29-31…Romans 8:35-39
- Measured by how we treat others…Matthew 10:42…Luke 6:37-38
- The focus of all God's laws……Mark 12:29-31
- Difficult to love if you only think of yourself…..Matthew 24:12
- Genuine vs. superficial….Mark 10:21f (2)
- Jesus loved the untouchable……Luke 5:13
- Loving your neighbor…..Luke 10-27-37f (2)
- Consistency of God's love…..Luke 15:20
- God sets the pattern for…..John 3:16
- God's love can change life's outcome……..John 13:27-38
- Why loving others is so important……John 13:34
- How do we love others as Christ loves us? …….John 15:12-13
- Love tied to obedience…..John 14:21
- Don't let small problems hinder yours…..John 15:17
- Jesus talks to Peter about…John 21:15-17f (2)
- Why it is the way to the Christian life..…..Romans 5:2-5
- Real love takes effort…..Romans 12:9
- Demonstrated when we forgive our enemies…..Roman 12:19-21
- Why is love for others called a debt? ….Romans 13:8
- The law of love…….Romans 13:10
- More important than spiritual gifts…..1 Corinthians 13:1ff
- What happens when we aren't motivated by love? …..Galatians 5:14-15
- God's love is total….Ephesians 8:17-19
- Husband commanded to love his wife…Ephesians 5:22-24f (2)
- How should a husband love his wife? ….Ephesians 5:25-30
- In family relationships….Ephesians 6:1-4
- Why Christians have no excuse for not loving others….Colossians 1:8
- God's discipline a sign of His love…….Hebrew 12:5-11
- Real love produces tangible actions…..Hebrew 13:1-5
- Can you love someone but still dislike them? …..1 John 2:9-11
- It is not what makes you feel good……1 John 4:8
- What motivates God love for us? ……1 John 4:9-10
- Spreads like fire……1 John 4:19
- Have you lost your zealous love for God? …..Revelation 2:4
- Loving people but not their sins…..Revelation 2:6f (2)

NOTES

My Story

Believing… Faith & Prayer..God has interceded

My story: a 20+ year old anger relationship with my dad

I was raised Christian, but drifted away from church and God in the 60's. As I mentioned earlier, there was a time that I did not believe in God; fortunately, during Bible classes I began to see life differently and "His Word" came alive to me. I grew up with many rules and He made it simply clear what the boundaries were. He set me free once I gave my heart to Jesus Christ. I was shocked what I was learning. I thought that the Bible was archaic; after all, we are so advanced today with all this new knowledge and technology, how could the Bible possibly help us today? I realized that people today still have the basic needs and wants that people had 2,000 years ago. Technology changed but people haven't. But..I ask you what good is knowledge, if one does not have the wisdom on how to use that knowledge wisely? While studying "The Word", I learned scripture is full of wisdom that enlivens the spirit, gets the creative juices moving in our minds and heart for production and growth.

Getting back to father:

I was angry at my dad before and after he and mother were divorced. It seemed to me that they argued all the time. Mother was alone for weeks at a time because dad's construction business covered western New York State. He was always traveling.

Now, years later I am married, living in Florida with two wonderful sons.

I had only spoken to my father once in 25 years. One day my sister called to tell me that my father was in the hospital recovering from a heart attack and that he had almost died. My thoughts were "That I did not know my own father. How sad!"

Than the decision was made, bought an airline ticket, made arrangements for a rental car and I called dad to tell him I was coming to visit. But first, I had to prepare myself mentally and emotionally to meet with him; because in the past, he always pressed my buttons and I always reacted. My goal was to have a conversation without any animosity and reaction. I began to pray while preparing myself. I

NOTES

attended Bible lessons, put faith in God; because with God all is possible. In Hebrews chapter 11 verse 1, "That faith is the substance of things hoped for, not yet seen, through faith in God."

I would lie in bed at night over and over again repeating this verse.

I was truly blessed; because at that time, I was in a great Bible class called Bible Study Fellowship (BSF). BSF is an intense Bible study that is given around the world. One big lesson that I had learned from one of my small discussion groups was how one scripture verse spoke to ten people in ten different ways and they each applied the lesson to their life in different ways. We are complex people and each having different needs in our life and God provides insights for each. What I learned from BSF is that God speaks to us as individuals to what we need at that moment in life. The Spirit of God is very creative and He is still creating. The way I see it when God puts the pieces together, it is better than my imagination…… and … I have a pretty wild imagination!

So I thought that I had everything together in preparing myself to meet my father. Inside, there was great determination to make this work and really get to know him. I would pray and study scripture so that I would <u>not react</u> to anything he would say. My heart was set on it. I was totally focused and looking forward to meeting with him.

Now it was the day that I was to fly to Buffalo. But first I had to attend BSF before catching my flight. I needed all the help that I could get. I had everyone in my small discussion group praying for me. Then all (about 250 people) met in the sanctuary, for a lecture, on the lesson for that week. The leader announced, "I am not going to cover today's lesson but had a special story to share with everyone." I thought it strange because they never go off format. The leader continued with a story of a man who was an atheist and had taken a six month personal leave from work to disprove the Bible. As he was critically researching the Bible, he became a "born again Christian." After this huge transformation in his life, he went to his father, who he had resented for years and asked for forgiveness. His father said, "Son, why a change in heart?" "Dad, I gave my life to Jesus Christ!"

The father said, "Son, if He can do that for you, than I give my heart to Christ too!" And they hugged for the very first time in years.

Well….the tears were streaming down my cheeks and I could not stop from crying. At the same time, I had to leave, it was getting late, and I had a flight to catch. I brought one of God's promise

NOTES

books with me to read on the flight. Everything went like clockwork. The flight was on time, rented a car, and drove two hours from Buffalo to a small town in Pennsylvania. Dad moved to Pennsylvania after the divorce. He had sold his property and construction business and lived in a tiny house in the hills and was there for 40 years. He left society and lived in the hills by himself with his books.

Dad knew I was coming to visit and I gave him an estimated time that I would arrive. I prayed as I knocked on his door. He opened it and the first thing he said, "Boy…did you get fat!"

Guess what I did? You guessed it…. <u>I reacted</u> and said, "Who needs this!"

I turned around to leave… and mentally I was already in Buffalo. I was going to leave as fast as my feet would take me. But…suddenly…hands gently touched my shoulders and turned me around…and …it was not my father! With that touch on my shoulder there was such a peace inside me that I never experienced before in my life. The whole environment in my dad's place had totally changed. I said to dad, "yes…I gained 30 lbs. and I love to eat!" We sat down and had a wonderful conversation for the very first time for 6 hours straight. I asked my dad questions about his family and childhood and talked a little about everything and anything. I did not know that my father was born in Pennsylvania and that he grew up in a mining town. His father, my grandfather, was killed in the mines when my dad was six years old. His mother was pregnant with her sixth child. His mother did not work and spoke Polish and did not speak a word of English. Soon after his father's death, his mother went away for the weekend, returned, and told the children that they were moving to Buffalo, New York. She just got married and they now had a step-dad and a new home. I looked at my father's face and I detected sadness and I believe that he never dealt with the death of his father. My father kept people at a distance; fortunately, I was getting to know him better. I had a great visit and there was no animosity or criticism. For the next ten years I would visit with my two sons so they could get to know their grandfather and dad could get to know his grandchildren.

He had developed prostate cancer; dad came down to Florida to visit and stayed with me. It was the first time that he had traveled in forty years. After returning to Pennsylvania he ended up in the emergency room. My sister called at 4 am, I hopped on an airplane and was at his bedside by 11:00 am. He looked shocked when I walked in and looked happy. He spent two days in intensive care and then in a coma for two days. I called the priest to Bless him and to give him his last rights. My sister,

NOTES

brother, and the priest stood around my father's bed and the priest spoke to my father for thirty minutes. It was an amazing time because the priest was also Polish and spoke to my father as if he was sitting up. He told my father how lucky he was to have his children with him. He told my father that God loved him and that God was with him. The priest called my father by name many times as if he was sitting up and listening. Dad had no movement for two days…but as the priest was talking my dad's head went from side to side and his chest heaved forward. I believe, at that moment, he had received the Holy Spirit. God's Blessings and Graces are always there when we need it most. Thank you Lord, Praise God for the Blessings!

NOTES

Dig Deep

NOTES

Digging Deeper for True Meaning

Deep Exploration

The following quote is taken from the book "The Sermon on the Mount – The Key to Success in Life" by Emmet Fox. Fox suggests using the following reflective study on "The Beatitudes, Sermon on the Mount," teachings of Jesus.

I suggest considering for all of scripture studies.

> "Do not imagine that you can assimilate all that it contains in one or two readings. It should be <u>gone over again and again</u> until you have thoroughly <u>grasped the scale of values</u> which the Sermon on the Mount presents to mankind. Only then will you experience the <u>New Birth.</u>
>
> The study of the Bible is <u>not</u> unlike the search for diamonds in South Africa. At first people found a few diamonds in the yellow clay, and they were delighted with their good fortune, even while they supposed that this was to be the full extent of their find.
>
> Then, upon digging deeper, they came upon the blue clay, and, to their amazement, they then found as many precious stones in a day as they had previously found in a year and what had formerly seemed like wealth faded into insignificance beside the <u>new riches</u>.
>
> In your <u>exploration</u> of Bible Truth, see to it that you <u>do not</u> rest satisfied in the yellow clay of a <u>few</u> spiritual discoveries, but press on to the <u>rich blue clay underneath</u>. The Bible, however, differs from the diamond field in the sublime fact that beneath the blue clay there are <u>more and still more and richer strata, awaiting the touch of spiritual perception.</u>"

Also from Fox:

> "He (Jesus) knew best about the art of living. The trouble and sorrow that humanity suffers are really due to the very fact that our mode of life is so opposed to the Truth." (p.26)

NOTES

Before Digging….

- This book is under 100 pages and point to point, with very little fill-ins. I have referenced other quality sources that get to the point of the matter.
- Important: To receive insights, I urge you to drop pre-conceived ideas, judgments, and biases, and reflect wholeheartedly on the text.

- God reveals truths: so go on a quest of discovery!
- He will reveal His character!
- If you have issues with your earthly father, I suggest not to judge God our Heavenly Father the same way.
- Reflect on each word and the messages within each diagram

- God will <u>un</u>cover and you will <u>dis</u>cover your unique beauty (reflections of God)
- At times we are our worst enemy, but you have a friend and counselor in Jesus Christ, who will help in many different, unique, and creative ways.
- Jesus paid the price for us. He will show you the way to the Father
- God, our creator is still creating. Trust, with "His Word," in that process of development

Study of Bible Scripture, an abundance of wealth…..a Real Treasure!

NOTES

You are the *Clay* in the *Potter's Hand!*

...."like clay" in the hand of the potter, so are you in My hand...Jeremiah 18:6 NIV

1. It is a process
2. Surrender to Jesus, making Him #1 in your life
3. Invite Him into your heart ♥
4. Pray continuously a daily walk with Jesus…moment to moment
5. Study the Bible: they are <u>not</u> just words on a piece of paper…………there is true meaning with<u>in</u> the words…dig deep and receive His treasure, awaiting you
6. Search for truths: "The truths will set you free"
7. Reflect/listen
8. Journal
9. With faith
10. The process is in now in progress!

Jesus Loves You!

Scripture says to <u>fear God</u>. Fear means to have <u>awesome respect</u> for God and all that He loves.

<u>Noah Webster 1828 Dictionary</u>: fear – to have a reverential awe…

Attention! Listen! Be wise, apply your heart! Faith!

NOTES

Listen

Proverbs 22:17-18 Bow down thine ear, and hear the words of the wise, and apply thine heart unto my knowledge. For it is a pleasant thing if thou keep them within thee…..KJV

Lectio Divina is:

Reflective meditation: "Listen with the ear of the Heart," attune to "His Word".

God loves you, He wants you to stand firm on a solid foundation, to be free, independent, and a life of purpose with continual growth. He will guide you…open your heart, focus on, and search for truths.

Suggestion: remove all distractions, read two or three lines, in silence, reflect, contemplate… pray. Record your thoughts in a journal.

God is Love

With Faith, there is Hope!

NOTES

Questions to Ponder and Answer before Journaling

Please write in a notebook your views on the following topics:

God	Peace of Mind? Do you have peace?
How do you picture God?	Justice – What does this mean to you?
What do you know about the Bible?	Truth – What is truth?
What do you think is a weak and strong foundation?	Holy Spirit – Have you experienced the power of the Holy Spirit?
What is Love?	What part of life is growth to you?
	What is maturity?

When journaling, remember that God is Love and God hates evil. Dig deep and reflect when studying scripture. It is not just words written on a piece of paper. There is great meaning, beauty, and knowledge of truth within "The Word".

You will see that we <u>cannot</u> live and grow to fullest maturity with knowledge of just a few scripture verses.

To receive the most value from this study, remember:

God is Love and you are His child adopted into His family when you wholeheartedly ♥ surrender to Jesus, believing, having faith in Him, inviting the Holy Spirit into your heart ♥, and God being #1 in your life.

NOTES

Foundation Building

Self-discovery

Self-government

NOTES

Ephesians 2:10 And are built upon the foundation of the apostles and prophets, Jesus Christ himself being the chief corner *stone*; KJV

Jesus spoke in Matthew 7:24-27 "Therefore everyone who hears these words of Mine, and acts upon them, may be compared to a wise man, who built his house upon the rock. And the rain descended, and the floods came, and the winds blew, and burst against that house; and yet it did not fall. For it had been founded upon the rock. "And everyone who hears these words of Mine, and does not act upon them, will be like a foolish man, who built his house upon the sand. "And the rain descended, and the floods came, and the winds blew and burst against that house; and it fell, and great was its fall." NASB

I Corinthians 10:4 ….and that Rock was Christ. KJV

Psalm 119:130 The unfolding of Thy words gives light; It gives understanding to the simple. NASB

NOTES

"Foundation of the Earth"

And, Thou, Lord, in the beginning hast laid the foundation of the earth.   Hebrews 1:10 KJV

Noah Webster's 1828 Dictionary….Foundation

3. The basis or ground-work, of anything; that on which anything stands, and by which it is supported. A free government has its *foundation* in the choice and consent of the people to be governed. Christ is the *foundation* of the church.

Behold, I lay in Zion for a *foundation,* a stone—a precious corner-stone. Is. 28.

Other *foundation* can no man lay than that which is laid, which is Jesus Christ. 1 Cor. 3.

4. Original; rise; as the *foundation* of the world.

Zechariah 12:1….The burden of the Word of the LORD for Israel, saith the LORD, which stretcheth forth the heavens, and layeth the foundation of the earth, and formeth the spirit of man within him….. KJV

Jesus spoke in Matthew 13:34-35 Jesus spoke all these things to the crowd in parables He did not say anything to them without using a parable. So it was fulfilled what was spoken through the prophet: "I will open my mouth in parables; I will utter things hidden since the creation of the world." NIV

Jesus spoke in Luke 6:49 But he that heareth, and doeth not, is like a man that without a foundation built a house upon the earth; against which the stream did beat vehemently, and immediately it fell; and the ruin of that house was great. KJV

NOTES

Foundation…. Basis….. Support

++Saul, of Tarsus, persecuted Christians. Afterwards; His spirit was transformed by the "Good News" of Jesus Christ, He had a change of heart ♥ and his name was changed to Paul. The rest of his life was preaching on the Words of Christ, his Savior. The following verses in the books of I Corinthians and Ephesians were written by Paul after his conversion.

<u>I Corinthians 3:10-13</u> By the grace God has given me, I laid a foundation as an expert builder, and someone else is building on it. But each one should be careful how he builds. For no one can lay any foundation other than the one already laid, which is Jesus Christ. If any man builds on this foundation using gold, silver, costly stones, wood, hay or straw, his work will be shown for what it is, because the Day will bring it to light. It will be revealed with fire, and the fire will test the quality of each man work. NIV

<u>Ephesians 2:19-20</u> Now therefore ye are no more strangers and foreigners, but fellow citizens with the saints, and of the household of God; And are built upon the foundation of the apostles and prophets, Jesus Christ himself being the chief corner stone; KJV

<u>Psalm 11:3</u> When the foundations are being destroyed, what can the righteous do? KJV

Building Blocks for a Strong Foundation

NOTES

Is God #1 in Your Life?

Otherwise; what is #1 in your life? What do you worship?

Who is your god (false god and idols worshipped)? Is it material things, money, another person, movie stars, yourself, the environment, are you moved by power, greed, manipulated games in life, etc.…etc.?

Isaiah 2:8 Their land also is full of idols; they worship the work of their own hands, that which their own fingers have made. KJV

Making God #1: He bestows His Blessings and Graces

Psalm 119:2 Blessed are they that keep his testimonies, and that seek him with the whole heart ♥. They also do no iniquity: they walk in his ways. KJV

Psalm 112:1 Praise ye the LORD. Blessed is the man that feareth the LORD, that delighteth greatly in his commandments. His seed shall be mighty upon earth: the generation of the upright shall be blessed. Wealth and riches shall be in his house: and his righteousness endureth for ever. Unto the upright there ariseth light in the darkness: he is gracious, and full of compassion, and righteous. A good man sheweth favour, and lendeth: he will guide his affairs with discretion. KJV

Fear the Lord – have awesome respect for Him!

NOTES

"Written in Stone"

"The Ten Commandments"   1445 – 1279 BC   *Located in the Old Testament*

And God spoke all these words:

"I am the Lord your God, who brought you out of Egypt, out of the land of slavery."

1. "You shall have no other gods before me."
2. "You shall not make for yourself an idol in the form of anything.."
3. "You shall not misuse the name of the Lord your God."
4. "Remember the Sabbath day by keeping it holy."

5. "Honor your father and your mother."
6. "You shall not murder."
7. "You shall not commit adultery.
8. "You shall not steal."
9. "You shall not give false testimony against your neighbor."
10. "You shall not covet your neighbor's house. You shall not covet your neighbor's wife, or his manservant or maidservant, his ox or donkey, or anything that belongs to your neighbor."

Exodus 20:1-17 NIV

NOTES

Blessed are They That Keep His Precepts!

Noah Webster's 1828 Dictionary…..Precept & Principle

PRE´CEPT

1. In a general sense, any commandment or order intended as an authoritative rule of action; but applied particularly to commands respecting moral conduct. The ten commandments are so many *precepts* for the regulation of our moral conduct.

PRIN´CIPLE [beginning]

I. In a general sense, the cause, source or origin of any thing; that from which a thing proceeds; as the principle of motion; the principles of action.   Dryden.

3. Being that produces any thing; operative cause.

   The soul of man is an active principle.   Tillotson.

5. Ground; foundation; that which supports an assertion, an action, or a series of actions or of reasoning. On what principle can this be affirmed or denied? He justifies his proceedings on the principle of expedience or necessity. He reasons on sound principles.

Psalm 119:2 Blessed are they who keep His statues, and seek Him with all their heart ♥.

Psalm 112:1 Unless the Lord builds the house, its builders labor in vain. KJV

Psalm 119:4 You have laid down precepts that are to be fully obeyed. KJV

NOTES

Know…by the Fruits They Produce!

> Jesus spoke in <u>Matthew 7:16-17</u> Ye shall know them by their fruits…….. Even so every good tree bringeth forth good fruit; but a corrupt tree bringeth forth evil fruit. A good tree cannot bring forth evil fruit; neither can a corrupt tree bring forth good fruit. KJV

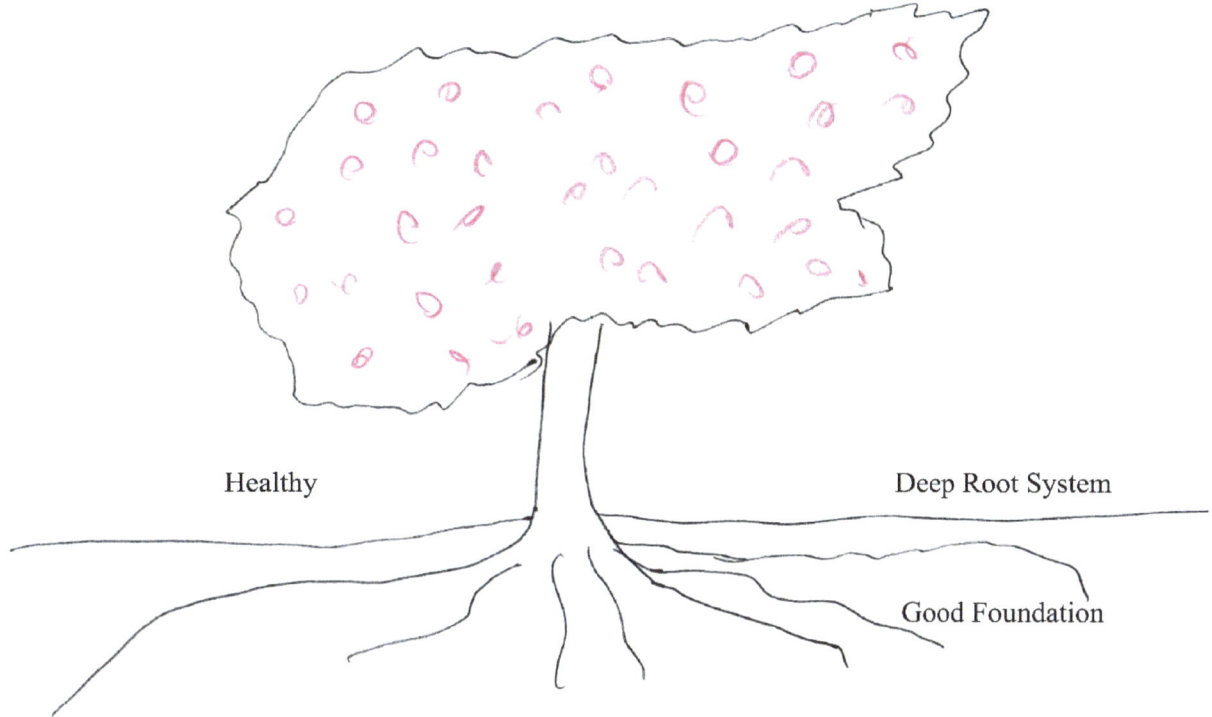

Healthy   Deep Root System

Good Foundation

He is the Tree of Life and He provides abundantly from a good and healthy foundation.

<u>Galatians 5:22-26</u> But the fruit of the Spirit is love, joy, peace, patience, kindness, goodness, faithfulness, gentleness and self control. Against such things there is no law. Those who belong to Christ Jesus have crucified the sinful nature with its passions and desires. Since we live by the Spirit, let us keep in step with the Spirit. Let us not become conceited, provoking and envying each other. NIV

> Jesus spoke in <u>Luke 8:15</u> "But that on the good ground are they, which in an honest and good heart ♥, having heard the word, keep it, and bring forth fruit with patience."

We bloom with Him!

NOTES

> Jesus spoke in <u>Matthew 7:18</u> …..neither *can* a corrupt tree bring forth good fruit. KJV

With a weaken root system, there is <u>no</u> fruit, because it lacks a poor foundation for growth.

> Jesus spoke in <u>Luke 6:45</u> A good man out of the good treasure of his heart ♥ bringeth forth that which is good; and an evil man out of the evil treasure of his heart ♥ bringeth forth that which is evil….. KJV

> Jesus spoke in <u>Matthew 15:13-14</u> He replied, "Every plant that my heavenly Father has not planted will be pulled up by the roots. Leave them they are blind guides. If a blind man leads a blind man, both will fall into a pit." NIV

Question to ponder – What type of seeds are you planting?

NOTES

Inner Man/Woman

Ephesians 3:16 That He would grant you, according to the riches of His glory, to be strengthened with might by His Spirit in the inner man; That Christ may dwell in your hearts ♥ by faith; that ye, being rooted and grounded in love. KJV

Noah Webster's 1828 on Education

Education - The bringing up, as of a child; instruction; formation of manners. Education comprehends all that series of instruction and discipline which is intended to enlighten the understanding, correct the temper, and form the manners and habits of youth, and fit them for usefulness in their future stations. To give children a good *education* in manners, arts and science, is important; to give them a religious *education* is indispensable; and an immense responsibility rests on parents and guardians who neglect these duties.

BEWARE!....Some curriculums could deaden and squelch the child's spirit. Find the method that will enliven their spirit that will give them excitement in learning and enlightenment while researching for truths.

Dr Montessori, a scientist and a Christian, spent her life studying child development with mentally challenged children, orphan children, and also normal of all races and cultures. Her methods with 2-6 yr. old were to enliven the spirit of the child and give nourishment to their souls.

Reflect on: If the spirit is numb, one could be operating by just intellectualizing or by operating from unresolved emotional feelings, or operating in automatic without any reflection of their behavior, events around them, and/or disregard to another person's boundaries.

A Christian education is vitally important when the method and instructions teach the "Word of God" in every area of life. Plant the seeds of character and continually developing with the "Word of the Lord," one building block at a time leads to maturity. The most important job in the world is raising children. I admire the parents who home school their children. They are totally committed to the type of information that is being fed into their child's mind. There are many unproductive and damaging forces that could steal the heart ♥ of the child.

Rosalie June Slater states that education should be a continual renewing of the mind. She was speaking of the Principle Approach method of teaching. This is America's historic Christian method of Biblical reasoning which makes "Truths of God's Word" the basis of every subject in the school curriculum. (Ages K-12 grade) This process opens minds and produces thinkers by reflective study through God's Word, the Bible, and Noah Webster's 1828 dictionary.

NOTES

The Hunter vs. the Farmer

Many years ago I read an article from two medical doctors that had Attention Deficit Disorder (ADD). (Don't you just love labels? This disorder sounds like it will never be in order) Back to the story… two doctors with ADD:

They believed thousands of years ago, for survival, there were two different personality types, the hunter and the farmer. The hunter had to search for food for his tribe. He is independent with unbelievable instincts, not only to hunt but to save himself from very dangerous animals and the environment. When he killed the animal, he would drag it back to the farmer type personality, the cultivator, to prepare the meat for eating, and the skins for clothing.

Our public school system today is set up for the farmer type personality that doesn't mind a routine schedule. I call this the 8 am to 5 pm type personalities who are good planners, focused, and conscious of time.

The hunter type is creative, loves visuals, hyper focuses, flexible, take risks, and likes highly stimulated activities. Many hate the farmer type school system and feel like a fish out of water. It is against their nature. The method of teaching should enliven <u>all</u> creative spirits instead of killing it.

http://www.thomhartmann.com/articles/2007/11/thom-hartmanns-hunter-and-farmer-approach-addadhd

By Dr. Thom Hartmann's book, "ADD: A Different Perception."

"How it appears in the "Hunter" view: Constantly monitoring their environment, able to throw themselves into the chase on a moment's notice, flexible; ready to change strategy quickly, tireless: capable of sustained drives, but only when "Hot on the trail" of some goal, visual/concrete thinker, clearly seeing a tangible goal even if there are not words for it, independent, bored by mundane tasks; enjoy new ideas, excitement, "the hunt" being hot on the trail, willing and able to take risk and face danger, "No time for niceties when there are decisions to be made!"

****Learn to learn again in a new way, by being inspired by "His Word". Build character values with a foundation of principles of knowledge and understanding with reasoning from His Great Textbook, "The Bible". God is still creating through His children.

NOTES

Do You Think We Should Judge a Book by Its Cover??

I Samuel 16:7

But the Lord said to Samuel, "Do not consider his appearance or his height, for I have rejected him. The Lord does not look at the things man looks at. Man looks at the outward appearance, but the Lord looks at the heart." ♥   NIV (1375-1220 BC)

External man/woman vs. *Internal man/woman*

⬇   ⬇

Superficial   vs. *Hidden self (the real person)*

The following quote: Emmet Fox referring to the (Old Law) Old Testament to the New Testament.

"The <u>Old Law</u>, dealing as it did with an earlier and <u>lower state</u> of the <u>race consciousness</u>, concerned itself necessarily with <u>external</u> things, for man's apparent evolution is from the outer to the inner; fundamental <u>spiritual growth is from inner to the outer</u>."

<u>Dear Christians add another tidbit from Emmet Fox:</u>

Fox viii "Conciseness of expression is the greatest assistance in mastering any subject."

<u>Noah Webster 1828 Dictionary……..conciseness</u>

Conciseness – brief, short, containing few words; comprehensive; the <u>principle</u> matters only.

<u>Ecclesiastes 12:12</u>….my son, be warned; the writing of many books is endless. And excessive devotion to books is wearying to the body. NASB

NOTES

Interior Man/Woman

Noah Webster's 1828 Dictionary……..interior

INTE´RIOR, *a* 1. <u>Internal</u>; being within any limits, inclosure or substance; inner; opposed to *exterior or superficial

> Jesus spoke in <u>Matthew 6:21</u> For where your treasure is, there will your heart ♥ be also. KJV

> Jesus spoke in <u>Matthew 5:8</u> Blessed *are* the pure in heart♥: for they shall see God. KJV

<u>Psalm 27:14</u> Wait on the Lord: be of good courage, and He shall <u>strengthen</u> thine heart… ♥ …KJV

<u>Jeremiah 29:13</u> And you shall <u>seek me</u>, and <u>find me</u>, when you <u>search for me</u> with <u>all your heart</u>. ♥ KJV

<u>I Kings 8:61</u> But your hearts ♥ must be fully committed to the Lord our God, to live by <u>His decrees</u> and obey His <u>commands</u>. KJV

<u>I Samuel 16:1</u> But the Lord said to Samuel, "Do <u>not</u> consider his appearances or his height, for I have rejected him. The Lord does <u>not</u> look at the things man looks at. Man looks at the outward appearance, but the <u>Lord looks at the heart</u>." ♥ KJV

NOTES

The Human Heart

Question to ponder: How does the condition of one's heart affect the results?

<u>Noah Webster's 1828 Dictionary…..heart</u>

4. The seat of the affections and passions, as of love, joy, grief, enmity, courage, pleasure.

The *heart* is deceitful above all things. Every imagination of the thoughts of the *heart* is evil continually. We read of an honest and good *heart*, and an evil *heart* of unbelief, a willing *heart*, a heavy *heart*, sorrow of *heart*, a hard *heart*, a proud *heart*, a pure *heart*. The *heart* faints in adversity, or under discouragement, that is, courage fails; the *heart* is deceived, enlarged, reproved, lifted up, fixed, established, moved.   *Scripture*.

5. By a metonymy, *heart* is used for an affection or passion, and particularly for love.

6. The seat of the understanding; as an understanding *heart*. We read of men wise in *heart*, and slow of *heart*.   *Scripture*.

7. The seat of the will; hence, <u>secret purposes</u>, <u>intentions</u> or designs. There are many devices in a man's *heart*. The *heart* of kings is unsearchable. The Lord tries and searches the *heart*. David had it in his *heart* to build a house of rest for the ark.   *Scripture*.

Sometimes *heart* is used for the will, or determined purpose.

The *heart* of the sons of men is fully set in them to do evil. Eccles. 8.

8. Person; character; used with respect to courage or kindness. Cheerily, my *hearts*.   *Shak.*

9. Courage; spirit; as, to take *heart*; to give *heart*; to recover *heart*.   *Spenser. Temple. Milton.*

10. Secret thoughts; recesses of the mind. Michal saw King David leaping and dancing before the Lord, and she despised him in her *heart*. 2 Sam 6.

11. Disposition of mind. He had a *heart* to do well.   *Sidney.*

***12. <u>Secret meaning; real intention</u>. And then show you the *heart* of my message.   *Shak.*

***13. <u>Conscience,</u> or sense of good or ill.

Every man's *heart* and conscience—doth either like or disallow it.   *Hooker.*

Do you know that the heart ♥ is mentioned over 1000x's in the Bible?

Why do you think the heart ♥ is so important?

NOTES

Grace

<u>Hebrews 13:9</u> Do not be carried away by all kinds of strange teachings. It is good for hearts ♥ to strengthen by grace…KJV

<u>Noah Webster's 1828 Dictionary….grace</u>

1. Favor; goodwill; kindness
2. Appropriately, the free <u>unmerited</u> love and favor of God, the spring and source of all the benefits men receive from Him. And by grace, it is more of works. Roman XI.
3. Favorable influence of God; divine influence or the influence of the Spirit in <u>renewing</u> the heart ♥ and restraining from sin.
   My grace is sufficient for thee. 2 Corinthians xii.
4. The application of Christ righteousness to the sinner.

   Where sin abound, <u>grace</u> did much more abound. Roman V.

♥

Heart and Thankfulness to the Lord

♥

<u>Colossians 3:15-17</u> And let the peace of God rule in your hearts, to which also ye are called in one body; and be ye thankful. Let the word of Christ dwell in you richly in all wisdom; teaching and admonishing one another in psalms and hymns and spiritual songs, singing with grace in your hearts ♥ to the Lord. And whatsoever ye do in word or deed, *do* all in the name of the Lord Jesus, giving thanks to God and the Father by him. KJV

NOTES

Connecting the Dots……..

Faith…Truth…Righteousness…Gospel of peace…Salvation…Supplication in the Spirit…

Noah Webster's 1828…..supplication

Supplication - 1. Entreaty; humble and earnest prayer in worship. In all our supplications to the Father of mercies, let us remember a world lying in ignorance and wickedness. 2. Petition; earnest request.

Hebrew 9:14 How much more shall the blood of Christ, who through the eternal Spirit offered himself without spot to God, purge your conscience from dead works to serve the living God? KJV

Hebrew 10:22 Let us draw near with a true heart♥ in full assurance of faith, having our hearts♥ sprinkled from an evil conscience and our bodies washed with pure water. KJV

Ephesians 6:14-18 Stand therefore, having your loins girt about with truth, and having on the breastplate of righteousness; And your feet shod with the preparation of the gospel of peace; Above all, taking the shield of faith, wherewith ye shall be able to quench all the fiery darts of the wicked. And take the helmet of salvation, and the sword of the Spirit, which is the word of God: Praying always with all prayer and supplication in the Spirit, and watching thereunto with all perseverance and supplication for all saints; KJV

Faith…Knowing…Believing

NOTES

Peace of Conscience

Noah Webster's 1828 Dictionary……..conscience

1. Internal or self-knowledge, or judgment of right and wrong; or the faculty, power or <u>principle within us</u>, which decides on the lawfulness or unlawfulness of our own actions and affections, and instantly approves or condemns them.

    Conscience is called by some writers the *moral sense,* and considered as an <u>original faculty of our nature</u>. Others question the propriety of considering conscience as a distinct faculty or principle. They consider it rather as the general principle of moral approbation or disapprobation, applied to one's own conduct and affections; alleging that our notions of right and wrong are not to be deduced from a single principle or faculty, but from various powers of the understanding and will.   *Encyc. Hucheson. Reid. Edin. Encyc.*

    Being convicted by their own *conscience,* they went out one by one. John 8.

    The *conscience* manifests itself in the feeling of obligation we experience, which precedes, attends and follows our actions.   *E. T. Fitch.*

    Conscience is first occupied in ascertaining our duty, before we proceed to action; then in <u>judging of our actions when performed</u>.   *J. M. Mason.*

2. The estimate or determination of conscience; justice; honesty.

    What you require cannot, in *conscience,* be deferred.   *Milton.*

3. Real sentiment; private thoughts; truth; as, do you in <u>*conscience* believe</u> the story?

With Faith, Search for Truth & Justice

There are many ways that peace is blocked:

1. *False idols – the worship of false gods: example; money, power, pride, ego (false sense of security), materialism……*
2. *Unresolved emotions*
3. *Lust……lust is not true love….lust will eventually fade*
4. *Collectivism – follows the collective mind (one should work on their own beliefs and stand as an individual, <u>to think on your own is freedom</u>)*
5. *Be aware of those with false messages!*

But with God our Creator, through scripture and with constant prayer, He is still creating, producing, building, and rebuilding.

NOTES

Truth

Noah Webster's 1828 Dictionary…..truth

1. Conformity to fact or reality; exact accordance with that which is, or has been, or shall be. The *truth* of history constitutes its whole value. We rely on the *truth* of the scriptural prophecies.

    My mouth shall speak *truth*. Prov. 8. Sanctify them through thy *truth;* thy word is *truth*. John 17.

2. True state of facts or things. The duty of a court of justice is to discover the *truth*. Witnesses are sworn to declare the *truth*, the whole *truth*, and nothing but the *truth*.

3. Conformity of words to thoughts, which is called *moral truth*.

    Shall *truth* fail to keep her word?   Milton.

4. Veracity; purity from falsehood; practice of speaking truth; habitual disposition to speak *truth*; as when we say, a man is a man of *truth*.

5. Correct opinion.   Harte.

7. Honesty; virtue. It must appear That malice bears down *truth*.   Shak.

9. Real fact or just principle; real state of things. There are innumerable *truths* with which we are not acquainted.

10. Sincerity.

    God is a spirit, and they that worship him must worship in spirit and in *truth*. John 4.

11. The *truth* of God, is his veracity and faithfulness. Ps. 71. Or his revealed will. I have walked in thy *truth*. Ps. 26.

12. Jesus Christ is called the *truth*. John 14.

13. ……………..*To do truth*, is to practice what God commands. John 3.

    Proverbs 3:21 My son, let them not depart from your sight; Keep sound wisdom and discretion. NASB

    Psalm 15:2 He who walks with integrity, and works righteousness and speaks truth in his heart ♥ . NASB

    John 4:24 God is spirit, and those who worship Him must worship Him in spirit and truth. NASB

> Jesus spoke in John 8:32 and you shall know the truth, and the truth shall make you free. NASB

    Ephesians 4:15 Instead, speaking the truth in love, we will in all things grow up into Him who is the Head, that is, Christ. NIV

Noah Webster 1828 Dictionary……preserve

    Preserve – to keep, to uphold, to save, to sustain (support, maintain) to defend from corruption.

NOTES

Truth ... Justice ... Faith

Noah Webster's 1828 Dictionary...Justice

2. The virtue which consists in giving to everyone what is his due; practical conformity to the laws and to principles of rectitude in the dealings of men with each other; honesty; integrity in commerce or mutual intercourse. *Justice* is *distributive* or *commutative*. *Distributive justice* belongs to magistrates or rulers, and consists in distributing to every man that right or equity which the laws and the principles of equity require; or in deciding controversies according to the laws and to principles of equity. *Commutative justice* consists in fair dealing in trade and mutual intercourse between man and man.

2. Impartiality; equal distribution of right in expressing opinions; fair representation of facts respecting merit or demerit. In criticisms, narrations, history or discourse, it is a duty to do *justice* to every man, whether friend or foe.

3. Equity; agreeableness to right; as, he proved the *justice* of his claim. This should, in strictness, be *justness*.

4. Vindictive retribution; merited punishment. Sooner or later, *justice* overtakes the criminal.

5. Right; application of equity. His arm will do him *justice*.

Isaiah 23+25 (Woe to those) who acquit the guilty for a bribe, but deny justice to the innocent. Therefore, the Lord's anger burns against His people; His hand is raised and strikes them down. NIV

Facing truth can sometimes be difficult and painful. It could be painful to learn when our wrong doings are exposed and uncovered. With God's Word, He will help us and guide us. If not, nature (cause & effect) will make those changes for us. The results could be worse and could set us back (backslide) 5, 10, 15 years. He wants to help His children. Surrender daily in prayer and study. He will guide you each step of the way. He is with you!

Progress, advance, move forward with the study of His Word!

Deuteronomy 16:18 Appoint judges and officials for each of your tribes in every town the Lord your God is giving you, and they shall judge the people fairly. Do not pervert justice or show partiality. Do not accept a bribe, for a bribe blinds the eyes of the wise and twists the words of the righteous. Follow justice and justice alone, so that you may live and possess the land the Lord our God is giving you.

Isaiah 51:4 "Listen to me, my people; hear me, my nation: The law will go out from me; My justice will become a light to the nations." NIV

Bribes Blind!

NOTES

Believing and Having Faith in God!

Noah Webster's 1828 Dictionary…faith

1. Belief; the assent of the mind to the truth of what is declared by another, resting on his authority and veracity, without other evidence; the judgment that what another states or testifies is the truth. I have strong *faith* or no *faith* in the testimony of a witness, or in what a historian narrates.

2. The assent of the mind to the truth of a proposition advanced by another; belief, on probable evidence of any kind.

3. In *theology*, the assent of the mind or <u>understanding</u> to the truth of what God has revealed. Simple belief of the scriptures, of the being and perfections of God, and of the existence, character and doctrines of Christ, founded on the testimony of the sacred writers, is called *historical* or *speculative faith*; a faith little distinguished from the belief of the existence and achievements of Alexander or of Cesar.

4. *Evangelical, justifying*, or *saving faith*, is the assent of the mind to the truth of divine revelation, on the authority of God's testimony, accompanied with a cordial assent of the will or approbation of the heart; an <u>entire confidence or trust in God's character and declarations</u>, and in the <u>character and doctrines of Christ</u>, with an unreserved surrender of the will to his guidance, and <u>dependence on his merits for salvation</u>. In other words, that <u>firm belief of God's testimony, and of the truth of the gospel</u>, which <u>influences</u> the will, and leads to an <u>entire reliance on Christ for salvation.</u>

    Being justified by *faith*. Rom. 5.

    Without *faith* it is impossible to please God. Heb. 11.

    For we walk by *faith*, and <u>not</u> by sight. 2 Cor. 5.

    With the *heart* man believeth to righteousness. Rom. 10.

    The *faith* of the gospel is that emotion of the mind, which is called trust or confidence, exercised towards the moral character of God, and particularly of the Savior.   *Dwight*.

    Faith is an affectionate practical confidence in the testimony of God.   *J. Hawes*.

    Faith is a firm, cordial belief in the veracity of God, in all the declarations of his word; or a full and affectionate confidence in the certainty of those things which God has declared, and because he has declared them.   *L. Woods*.

5. The object of belief; a doctrine or system of doctrines believed; a system of <u>revealed truths received by Christians</u>. They heard only, that he who persecuted us in times past, now preacheth the *faith* which once he destroyed. Gal. 1.

6. The promises of God, or his truth and faithfulness.

    Shall their unbelief make the *faith* of God without effect? Rom. 3.

7. An open profession of gospel truth.

    Your *faith* is spoken of throughout the whole world. Rom. 1.

NOTES

...Resolution...Obscurity...Victory...

Noah Webster's 1828 Dictionary...Resolution

<u>Resolution</u> (2) The act or process of <u>un</u>raveling or <u>dis</u>entangling perplexities or of dissipating obscurity in moral subjects, as the resolution of difficult questions in moral science.

...Obscurity...

<u>Obscurity</u> - darkness; want of light.

"We wait for light, but behold obscurity." Isaiah 1ix.

(3) Darkness of meaning; unintelligibleness; as the obscurity of writings.

...Victory...

<u>Victory</u> – conquer (2) The advantage or superiority gained over spiritual enemies, or passions and appetites, or over temptations, or any struggle or competition. "Thanks be to God, who giveth us the victory, through our Lord Jesus Christ. I Corinthians XV.

The victory is in the process of learning the right & proper knowledge that leads to wisdom!

Some men and women just intellectualize and leave out the heart♥. With God, His Holy Spirit within our hearts♥ and His Word, there is Wisdom & discernment. He heals the broken and harden hearts♥. What we do today, with or without Him, will impact the future....and children's future......cause/effect/consequence.

<u>Romans 3:22-25</u> Even the righteousness of God *which is* by faith of Jesus Christ unto all and upon all them that believe: for there is no difference: For all have sinned, and come short of the glory of God; Being justified freely by his grace through the redemption that is in Christ Jesus: Whom God hath set forth *to be* a propitiation through faith in his blood, to declare his righteousness for the remission of sins that are past, through the forbearance of God;

<u>Ephesians 6:16</u> ...taking up the shield of faith with which you will be able to extinguish all the flaming missiles of the evil one. NASB

NOTES

Four (4) Sides to Man/Woman

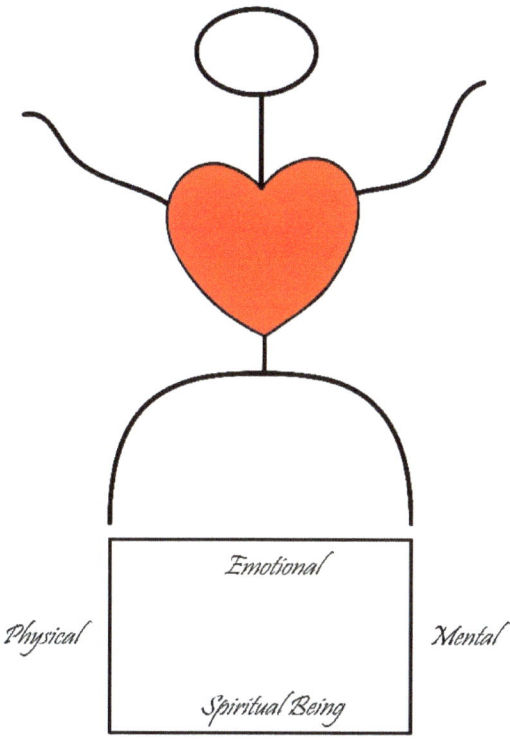

Noah Webster's 1828 Dictionary……..being

Existence; as, God is the author of our *being*.

> In God we live, and move, and have our *being*. Acts 17.

3. A person existing; *applied to the human race*.

4. An immaterial, intelligent existence, or spirit.

> Superior *beings*, when of late they saw
>
> A <u>mortal</u> man <u>unfold all nature's law</u>—   Pope.

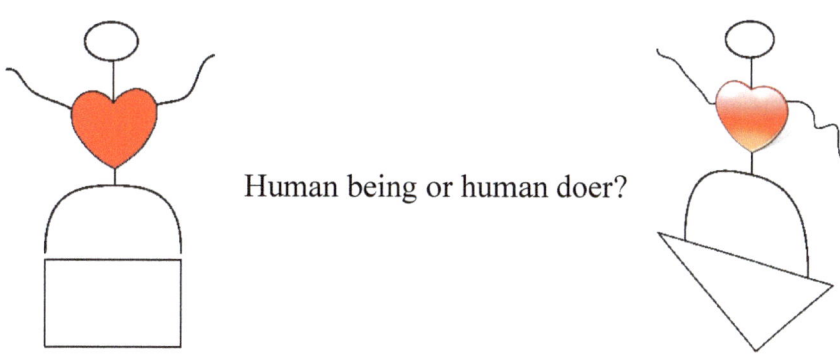

Human being or human doer?

NOTES

Spiritual Side of Man/Woman

With Him, there is life, light, growth, development, and maturity. He wants us to continually build on this foundation with Him, one brick at a time, one principle at a time. Reflecting on it, living it, growing with His precepts; He wants to help and assist us to developing good fruits and to be productive individuals.

Self-discipline/Self-government

NOTES

Light vs. Darkness

Light/Biblical worldview

Principles/Life/Wholeness/Harmony

Darkness/worldview

The world's way

One side of nature is missing

Noah Webster's 1828 Dictionary……whole

Whole

2. Complete; entire;

5. Restored to health and soundness; sound; well.

  Thy <u>faith</u> hath made thee whole. Mark 5.

<u>Romans 12:2</u> And be not conformed to this world: but be ye transformed by the renewing of your mind, that ye may prove what *is* that good, and acceptable, and perfect, will of God. KJV

He intercedes with His Spirit within. He transforms with new growth, new life, one revelation at a time, for better understanding, and clearer thinking. We grow with knowing, studying, digesting, and being inspired through "His Word".

NOTES

Darkness

<u>John 1:3</u> All things were made by Him; and without Him was not any thing made that was made. In Him was life; and the life was the light of men. And the light shineth in darkness; and the darkness comprehended it not. KJV

Moved by un-forgiveness (anger/hurt/rebellion)
Moved by misplaced emotions
Moved by controlling others
Moved by power/Control
Self-deception/ Greed
Guilt or Shame
Fear
Etc.

Darkness/Worldview

Concretized in their hearts ♥, mind, and thought pattern....possibly forever....suppressing the truth. I believe that if we are separated from God on earth, we will be separated from Him in all eternity.

NOTES

After their own Lusts and far away from Sound Doctrine

2 Timothy 4:3-4 For the time will come when they will not endure sound doctrine; but after their own lusts shall they heap to themselves teachers, having itching ears; And they shall turn away *their* ears from the truth, and shall be turned unto fables. KJV

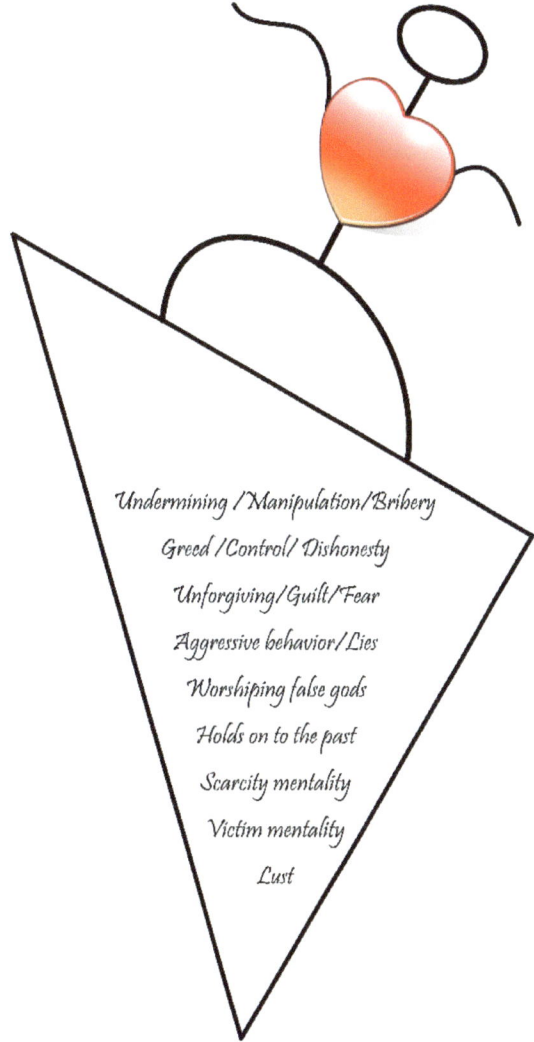

Undermining /Manipulation/Bribery
Greed /Control/ Dishonesty
Unforgiving/Guilt/Fear
Aggressive behavior/Lies
Worshiping false gods
Holds on to the past
Scarcity mentality
Victim mentality
Lust

Darkness/Immaturity/Lack standards/Disregards boundaries
Condemned by his/her own foolishness
Dis-ease=disease

Jesus spoke in Luke 5:33 Jesus answered, "It is not the healthy who need a doctor, but the sick. I have not come to call the righteous, but sinners to repentance." NIV

NOTES

A Foundation that Leads to Wisdom

Ephesians 1:7+8 In Him we have redemption through His blood, the forgiveness of sins in accordance with the riches of God's grace that He lavished on us all wisdom and understanding. NIV

God's Great Textbook "THE BIBLE"

Noah Webster's 1828 Dictionary

A person could have a lot of knowledge, but without wisdom, what good is that knowledge?

With God's Word….Wisdom grows! Understanding! Discernment!

Help yourself and study the Word of God. Seek to walk in His presence, have conversations with the Lord like you would with a close friend. Make sure there is quiet time away from all the busyness and meditate on His Word and listen. Listen…everything good and loving is from God. If there are negative thoughts, ask the Lord to show and keep you in good, loving thoughts and ways. Grow in inspiration from the Bible and utilizing Noah Webster's 1828 Christian Dictionary, attend Bible classes, or start a home Bible class.

Psalm 18:1-2 I love you, O Lord, by strength. The Lord is my rock, my fortress and my deliverer; my God is my rock, in whom I take refuge. KJV

2 Timothy 3:16 All Scripture is God-breathed and is useful for teaching, rebuking, correcting, and training in righteousness, so that the man of God may be thoroughly equipped for every good work. NIV

NOTES

Discernment and Wisdom

Noah Webster's 1828 Dictionary.........**Discernment**.....

The act of discerning; also, the power or faculty of the mind, by which it distinguishes one thing from another, as truth from falsehood virtue from vice; acuteness of judgment; power of perceiving differences of things or ideas, and their relations and tendencies. The errors of youth often proceed from the want of *discernment*.

.......**WIS′DŎM**......

1. The right use or exercise of knowledge; the choice of laudable ends, and of the best means to accomplish them. This is wisdom in *act, effect,* or *practice.* If wisdom is to be considered as a *faculty* of the mind, it is the faculty of discerning or judging what is most just, proper and useful, and if it is to be considered as an *acquirement,* it is the knowledge and use of what is best, most just, most proper, most conducive to prosperity or happiness. Wisdom in the first sense, or *practical wisdom,* is nearly synonymous with *discretion.* It differs somewhat from *prudence,* in this respect; *prudence* is the exercise of sound judgment in avoiding evils; *wisdom* is the exercise of sound judgment either in avoiding evils or attempting good. *Prudence* then is a species, of which *wisdom* is the genus.

   Wisdom gained by experience, is of inestimable value.   *Scott.*

   It is hoped that our rulers will act with dignity and *wisdom;* that they will yield everything to reason, and refuse everything to force.   *Ames.*

4. Natural instinct and sagacity. Job 39.

5. In *Scripture theology,* wisdom is true religion; godliness; piety; the knowledge and fear of God, and sincere and uniform obedience to his commands. This is the *wisdom* which is from above. Ps. 90. Job 28.

I repeat Emmet Fox,

"Conciseness of expression is the greatest assistance in mastering any subject."

N. Webster's 1828.......**Conciseness**......

Brief, short, containing <u>few</u> words; comprehensive; the <u>principle</u> matters only

NOTES

Secrets to Wisdom

Advice from Solomon (around 1000 -935 BC), one of the richest and wisest of men wrote Proverbs for leading a Godly life.

<u>I Kings 10:24</u> The whole world sought audience with Solomon to hear the <u>wisdom</u> God had put in his heart ♥. KJV

WISDOM FOR YOUNG PEOPLE

<u>Proverbs 1:1-7</u> The proverbs of Solomon son of David, king of Israel:

for attaining wisdom and discipline;

for understanding words of insight;

for acquiring a disciplined and prudent life,

doing what is right and just and fair;

for giving prudence to the simple,

knowledge and discretion to the young-

let the wise listen and add to their learning,

and let the discerning get guidance-

for understanding proverbs and parables,

the saying and riddles of the wise.

the fear of the Lord is the beginning of knowledge,

but fools despise wisdom and discipline. NIV

Spiritual gifts & promises: attaining wisdom, discipline, understanding, insight, prudence, discretion, and guidance from the Holy Spirit = the road to growth, maturity, and productivity.

NOTES

Wisdom & Understanding

Proverbs 3:13-23 NIV

13. How blessed is the man who finds wisdom,

And the man who gains understanding.

14. For its profit is better than the profit of silver,

And its gain than fine gold.

15. She is more precious than jewels;

And nothing you desire compares with her.

16. Long life is in her right hand;

In her left hand are riches and honor.

17. Her ways are pleasant ways,

And all her paths are peace.

18. She is a tree of life to those who take hold of her,

And happy are all who hold her fast.

19. The Lord by wisdom founded the earth;

By understanding He established the heavens.

20. By His knowledge the deeps were broken up,

And the skies drip with dew.

21. Nothing my son, let them not depart from your sight;

Keep sound wisdom and discretion,

22. So they will be life to your soul,

And adornment to your neck.

23. Then you will walk in your way securely,

And your foot will not stumble.

NOTES

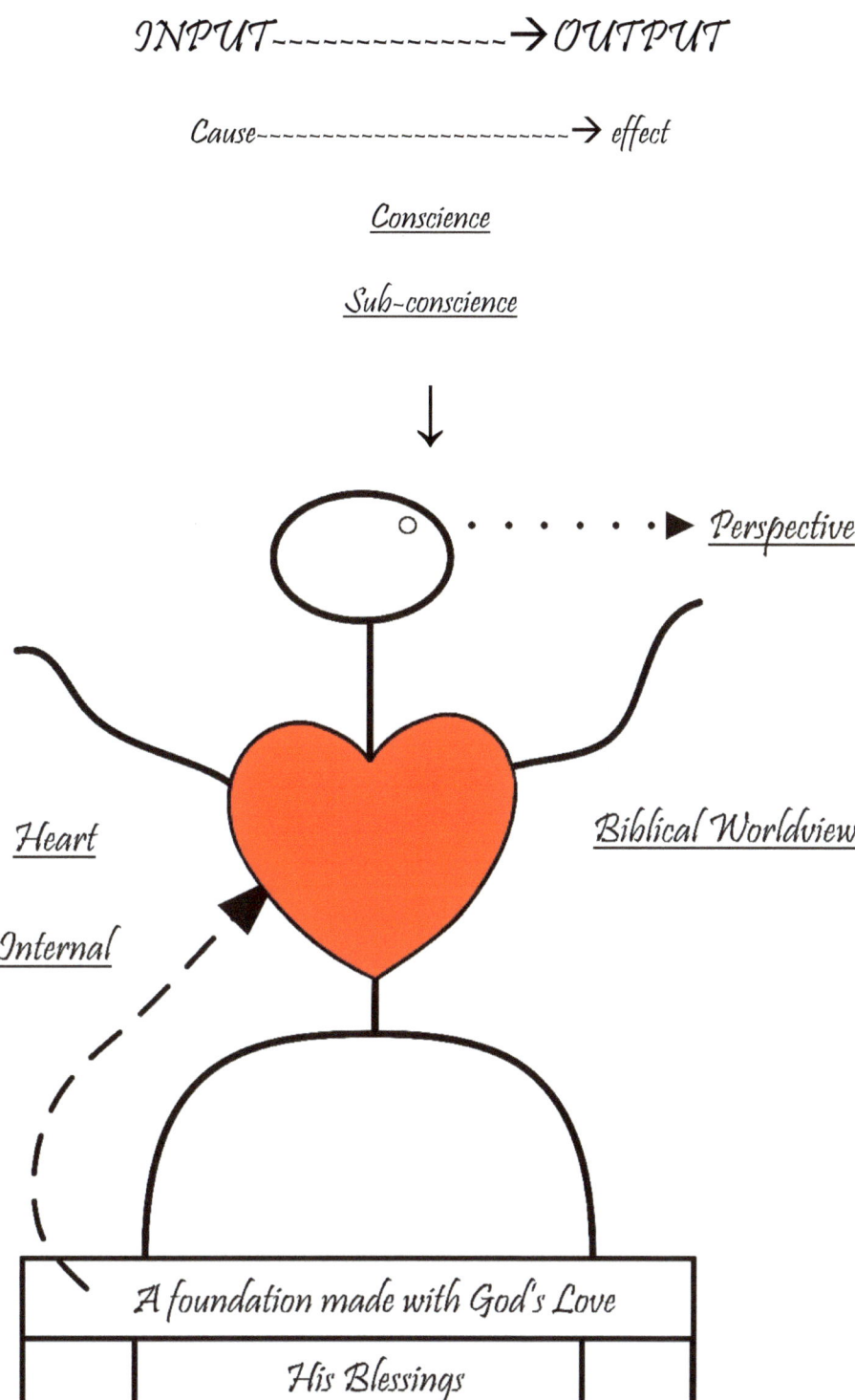

NOTES

MAKE GOD THE CAUSE

The cause will determine the results

N. Webster's 1828 Dictionary....<u>cause</u>......

2. That which produces an effect; that which impels into existence, or by its agency or operation produces what did not before exist; that by virtue of which any thing is done; that from which any thing proceeds, and without which it would not exist.

Cause is a substance exerting its power into act, to make a thing begin to be.   *Locke.*

3. The reason or motive that urges, moves, or impels the mind to act or decide.

6. *Without cause*, without good reason; without a reason or motive to justify the act.

They hate me *without cause.* Ps. 35:19.

NOTES

Effect

Noah Webster's 1828 Dictionary………effect

EFFECT', *v. t.* [from the Noun.] To produce, as a cause or agent; to cause to be.

2. To bring to pass; to achieve; to accomplish; as, to *effect* an object or purpose.

CAUSE-------------------→ *EFFECT*------------------→*CONSEQUENCE*

INPUT---→ *OUTPUT*

Galatians 3:3 Are you so foolish? After beginning with the Spirit, are you now trying to attain your goal by human effort? (4) Have you suffered so much for nothing – if it really was for nothing? (5) Does God give you His Spirit and work miracles among you because you observe the law, or because you believe what you heard? NIV

***Grow with Spirit and the Spirit is active and productive. ***Are you a human being or just a human doer?

*Work and lead productive lives with the Spirit. **With Him, creativity and production of good fruits.

Be inspired * Be in-spirit * invite His Spirit into your heart ❤ ! His Spirit dwells within each believer.

*The Spirit is creative and produces out of the box thinkers and reflectors with new and refreshing creative ways. You never know which way the wind is going to blow, with faith, and in His word,

> Jesus spoke in John 3:3 Jesus answered and said unto him, Verily, verily, I say unto thee, Except a man be born again, he cannot see the kingdom of God.
>
> Jesus spoke in John 3:6 That which is born of the flesh is flesh; and that which is born of the Spirit is spirit.
>
> Jesus spoke in John 4:23 But the hour cometh, and now is, when the true worshippers shall worship the Father in spirit and in truth: for the Father seeketh such to worship him. 24 God *is* a Spirit: and they that worship him must worship *him* in spirit and in truth.

2 Corinthians 5:7 Therefore *we are* always confident, knowing that, whilst we are at home in the body, we are absent from the Lord: 7 (For we walk by faith, not by sight:)

Psalm 18:30 *As for* God, his way *is* perfect: the word of the LORD is tried: he *is* a buckler to all those that trust in him. 31 For who *is* God save the LORD? or who *is* a rock save our God? 32 *It is* God that girdeth me with strengthand maketh my way perfect.

Psalm 118:8 *It is* better to trust in the LORD than to put confidence in man. (All above KJV)

NOTES

The Bible

The Bible has many stories regarding cause, effect, and consequences that can occur in many different life situations. Man has not changed, technology has. Man still has the same basic needs and wants that man had 2,000 years ago.

The Bible is the Great Textbook to building a strong foundation, to sharpen awareness and the conscience, to set boundaries for one-self and at the same time learn to respect other people's boundaries. With knowledge of His Word, there is continual growth, a process that transforms one through daily surrender, daily rebirth. God shares His Glory and Graces with us every step of the way. Yes, get to know God and His word 24/7 in all areas of life. Stay connected, study His word, and pray for the indwelling guidance from the Holy Spirit within.

Invite the Holy Spirit into your heart.......ASK in prayer.

Ask-----→ Seek---→ Knock

Jesus spoke in Matthew 7:7 Ask, and it shall be given you; seek, and ye shall find; knock, and it shall be opened unto you: 8 For every one that asketh receiveth; and he that seeketh findeth; and to him that knocketh it shall be opened. KJV

Inspiration/be inspired /in-spirit

NOTES

Common Sense is NOT so Common!

They only know what they see…they only see what they know!

Subconscious habits
Behavior patterns in automatic

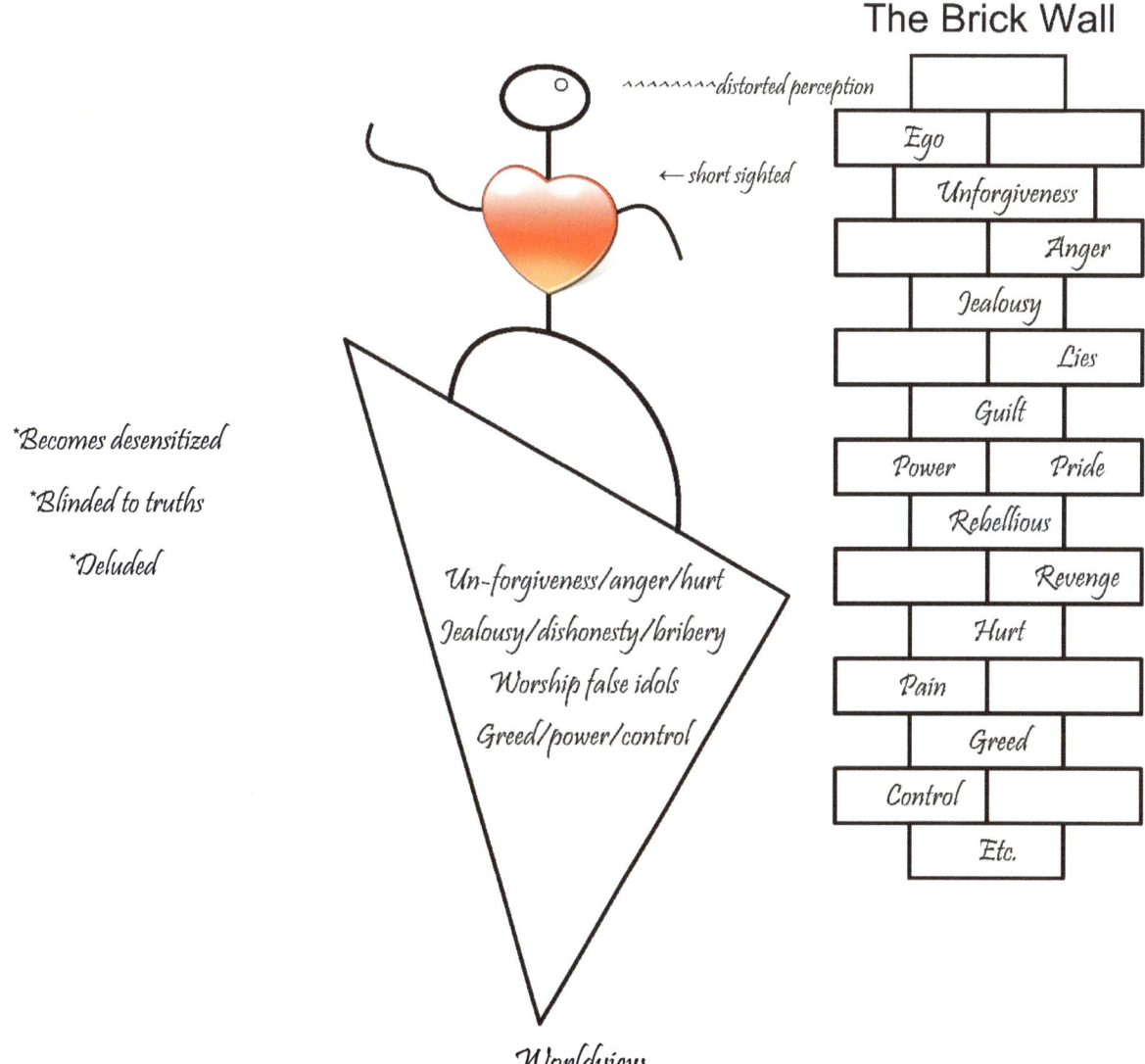

Isaiah 5:21 Woe to those who are wise in their own eyes, and clever in their own sight. NIV

Sin is against God's Love Nature

NOTES

They only know what they see!

*They only know what they **want** to see!*

Their own delusions!

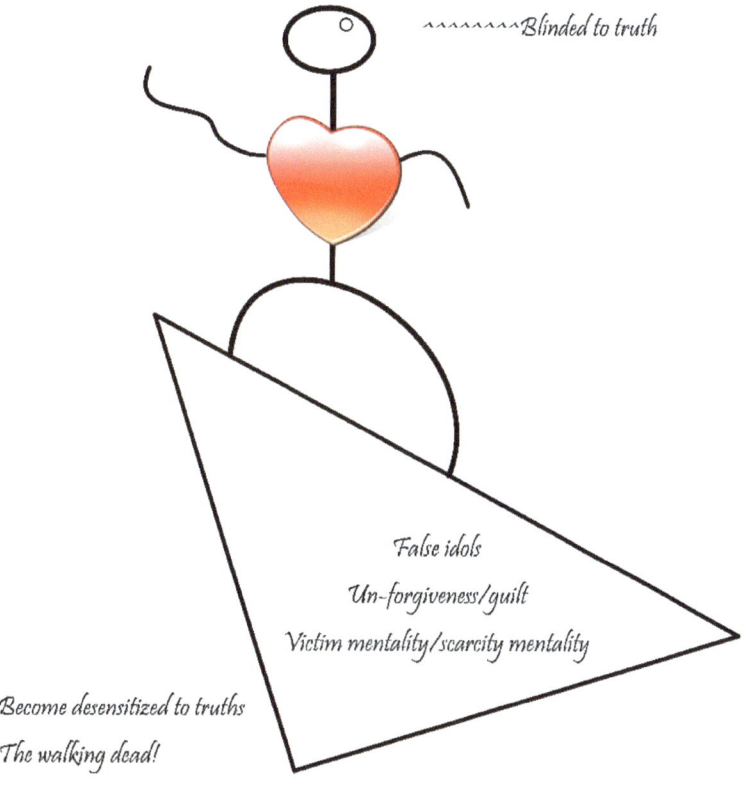

Ephesians 2:1 …you were dead in your transgressions and sins…when you followed the ways of the world…. NIV

I Corinthians 10:23 "Everything is permissible", but not everything is beneficial. "Everything is permissible", but not everything is constructive. NIV

Ephesians 4:18-19 They are <u>darkened</u> in their understanding and <u>separated</u> from the life of God because of the <u>ignorance</u> that is in them due to the <u>hardening of their hearts</u> ♥. Having <u>lost all</u> <u>sensitivity</u>, they have given <u>themselves over to sensuality</u> so as to indulge in <u>every kind of</u> <u>impurity</u>, with a <u>continual lust for more</u>.

Thirst for more, they will never be satisfied. It is like a drug. Are they free? Freedoms come with accountability and personal responsibility. If an individual cannot self-govern themselves, they could be controlled by passion and misplaced emotions. Is this freedom? Are they really free?

With God and "His Word", He releases those bondages that don't serve us well!

NOTES

<u>Bondage</u>

Footholds = bondages = strongholds = yolk of slavery

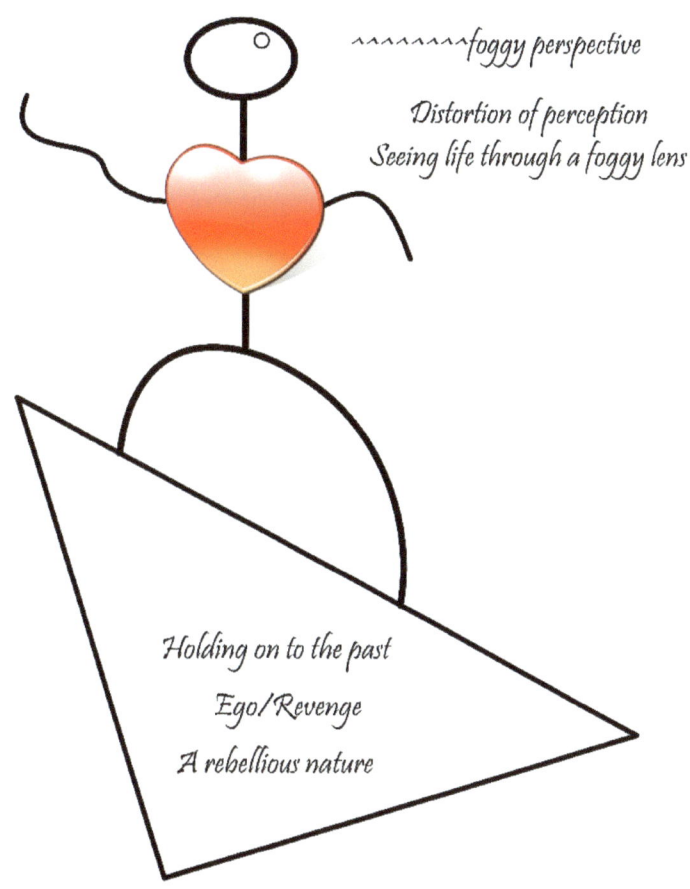

foggy perspective

Distortion of perception
Seeing life through a foggy lens

Holding on to the past
Ego/Revenge
A rebellious nature

Some patterns (good & bad) are past down from one generation to the next, now buried deep in the sub-conscious

Disorder/Out of order

Lack of standards/deluded

Not free/bondage/immaturity

Jesus spoke in <u>Matthew 24:4</u> *"See to it that no one misleads you."*

NOTES

The Yoke of Bondage

Psalm 130:3+4 If you, O Lord, kept a record of sins, Oh Lord, who could stand? But with you there is forgiveness. NIV

Psalm 4:2 How long, O men, will you turn my glory into shame? How long will you love delusions and seek false gods? NIV

Roman 8:15 For ye have not received the spirit of bondage again to fear; but ye have received the Spirit of adoption, whereby we cry, Abba, Father. [16] The Spirit itself beareth witness with our spirit, that we are the children of God: KJV

Galatians 5:1 Stand fast therefore in the liberty wherewith Christ hath made us free, and be not entangled again with the yoke of bondage. KJV

Question to ponder:

If an individual cannot self-govern themselves, what are they controlled by? Are they controlled by passions, lust, or misplaced emotions etc.? Is this freedom? Are they really free?

With Him, He releases those bondages, the yoke of slavery. He not only released the Jews from slavery from Egypt, He releases us from ourselves.

NOTES

| Jesus spoke in Matthew 6:23 "…how great *is* that darkness!" KJV |

Warning!

2 Timothy 3:13 But evil men and impostors will proceed from bad to worse, deceiving and being deceived. NASB

Ephesians 5:11… do not participate in the unfruitful deeds of darkness, but instead even expose them. NASB

Psalm 107:10 There were those who dwelt in darkness and in the shadow of death, prisoners in misery and chains. NASB

NOTES

Men/Women Love Darkness

> Jesus spoke in John 3:19-21 "This is the verdict: Light has come into the world, but men loved darkness instead of light because their deeds were evil. Everyone who does evil hates the light, and will not come into the light for fear that his deeds will be exposed. But whoever lives by the truth comes into the light, so that it may be seen plainly that what he has done has been done through God. NIV

The first time I faced my evil deeds, it was painful and embarrassing; but with prayer and meditation on His Word and believing in Him, the Truth set me free!

I John 1:8-10 If we claim to be without sin, we deceive ourselves and the truth is NOT in us. If we confess our sins, He is faithful and just and will forgive us or sins and purify us from all unrighteousness. If we claim we have not sinned, we make Him out to be a liar and His work has no place in our lives. NIV

He releases the guilt from our past; ask Jesus for release by forgiveness. He knows the attitude of our hearts *!*

He removes the darkness and brings in the light… there is new birth…transformation!

Proverbs 10:25 When the storm has swept by, the wicked are gone, but the righteous stand firm forever. NIV

Isaiah 9:4…you have shattered the yoke that burdens them, the bar across their shoulders, the rod of their oppressor. NIV

Isaiah 9:2 The people walking in the darkness have seen a great light; on those living in the land of the shadow of death a light has dawned. NIV

> Jesus spoke in Acts 26:18 "To open their eyes so that they may turn from darkness to light and from the dominion of Satan to God, in order that they may receive forgiveness of sins and an inheritance among those who have been sanctified by faith in Me." NASB

Luke 1:79 "…to shine on those living in darkness and in the shadow of death, to guide our feet into the path of peace." NIV

Things concealed; but in believing and addition with an open heart…He, the Lord reveals!

NOTES

From Babe to Maturity

<u>Hebrews 5:11-14</u> Concerning Him we have much to say, and it is hard to explain, since you have become dull of hearing. For though by this time you ought to be teachers, you have need again for someone to teach you the elementary principles of the oracles of God, and you have come to need milk and not solid food. For everyone who partakes only of milk is not accustomed to the word of righteousness, for he is a babe. But solid food is for the mature, who because of <u>practice have their senses trained to discern good and evil</u>. NASB

<u>mature</u>; complete (in various areas of labour, growth, mental and moral character etc.) NASB Hebrew section: (p.2290)

<u>babe</u>; metaphorically: a babe, one unlearned, unenlightened, simple, innocent. (Mt 21:16; 1Co 13:11) NASB Hebrew section: (p.2228)

<u>senses</u>; internal sense, faculty of perception. NASB Hebrew section: (p.2086)

> Jesus spoke in <u>Mark 4:26-29</u> And He was saying, "The kingdom of God is like a man who casts seed upon the soil; and goes to bed at night and gets up by day, and the seed sprouts up and grows--how, he himself does not know. The soil produces crops by itself; first the blade, then the head, then the mature grain in the head. But when the crop permits, he immediately puts in the sickle, because the harvest has come." NASB

<u>2 Corinthians 13:8-14</u> For we can do nothing against the truth, but only for the truth. For we rejoice when we ourselves are weak but you are strong; this we also pray for, that you be made complete. For this reason I am writing these things while absent, in order that when present I may not use severity, in accordance with the authority which the Lord gave me, for <u>building up</u> and <u>not for tearing down</u>. Finally, brethren, rejoice, be made complete, be comforted, be like-minded, live in peace; and the God of love and peace shall be with you. Greet one another with a holy kiss. All the saints greet you. Christ, and the love of God, and the fellowship of the Holy Spirit, be with you all. NASB

NOTES

He sets us free!

- *A.S.K., and have conversation with God, the things upon your heart ♥!*

<u>I John 1:5</u> And this is the message we have heard from Him and announce to you, that God is light, and in Him there is no darkness at all.

<u>Isaiah 49:9-10</u> "to say to the captives, "Come out" and to those in darkness, "Be free!" "They will feed beside the roads and find pasture on every barren hill. They will neither hunger nor thirst…" NIV

The first time I recognized my sins it was painful. It was painful for me to reflect on my own behavior. My sins were exposed. Some sins were passed down from generation to generation. At the time, I felt like the walking dead! I was in bondage.

Thank the Lord, He gives a new life! He continually shows me a new way!

<u>Psalm 130:3-4</u> If thou, LORD, shouldest mark iniquities, O Lord, who shall stand? ⁴ But *there is* forgiveness with thee, that thou mayest be feared. KJV

++Fear means awesome respect

- *Remember:* **God is Love**….*If it is not love, than what is it?*

> Jesus spoke in <u>John 3:21</u> "But he that doeth truth cometh to the light, that his deeds may be made manifest, that they are wrought in God." KJV

<u>Romans 12:2</u> And be not conformed to this world: but be ye transformed by the renewing of your mind, that ye may prove what *is* that good, and acceptable, and perfect, will of God. KJV

<u>Leviticus 26:13</u> I am the Lord your God, who brought you out of Egypt so that you would no longer be slaves to the Egyptians; I broke the bars of your yoke and enabled you to walk with heads held high. NIV

In the book of Leviticus, Moses, 1445 BC (Before Christ), spoke on freedom and freed his people that were enslaved.

Search for truths…and the truth will set you free!

NOTES

God Molds Strong Character Traits!

Learn the nature of God by learning the character of Jesus Christ!

Invite the Holy Spirit into your heart ♥

Reflective study
Sharpens awareness
Growth
Maturity
Salvation
Eternal Life

Building Blocks
Creates value
Productive/enterprising

God's Word

Principles

Love, faith, hope

Cause

He provides order and structure in all areas of life

<u>Psalm 19:7</u> The law of the LORD is perfect, converting the soul: the testimony of the LORD *is* sure, making wise the simple. The statutes of the LORD are right, rejoicing the heart ♥ : the commandment of the LORD *is* pure, enlightening the eye. KJV

<u>1Timothy 4:11-12</u> Command and teach these things. Don't let anyone look down on you because you are young, but set an example for the believers in speech, in life, in love, in faith, and in purity. NIV

NOTES

Renewal of Friendship…New Creation in Christ Jesus

- ✓ *It is a process*
- ✓ *Surrender to Jesus*
- ✓ *Invite Him into your heart* ♥
- ✓ *Ask the Holy Spirit for guidance*
- ✓ *Pray*
- ✓ *Study the Bible (they are not just words on a piece of paper…………there is true meaning within/behind the words…dig deep and receive His treasure awaiting you)*
- ✓ *Reflect/listen*
- ✓ *Journal*
- ✓ *Progress is in the process!*

Therefore, if anyone is in Christ, he is a new creation; the <u>old has gone</u>, the <u>new has come</u>! All this is from <u>God who reconciled us to Himself through</u> Christ and gave us the ministry of reconciliation: that God was reconciling the <u>world to Himself in Christ</u>, **not** counting men's sins against them. And He has committed to us the message of reconciliation. <u>2 Corinthians 5:17-18</u> NIV

Noah Webster 1828 Dictionary……<u>reconciliation</u>

1. The act of reconciling parties at variance; renewal of friendship after disagreement or enmity.

    Reconciliation and <u>friendship with God</u>, really form the basis of all rational and true enjoyment.   *S. Miller.*

2. In *Scripture*, the means by which sinners are reconciled and brought into a <u>state of favor with God</u>, after natural estrangement or enmity; the atonement; expiation.

Being attentive, listen, be wise, and watch the attitude of your heart ♥ *!*

<u>Proverbs 22:17</u> Bow down thine ear, and hear the words of the wise, and apply thine heart ♥ unto my knowledge. KJV

NOTES

Warning....Thoughts have Power!

<u>*Deuteronomy 15:9*</u> Beware that there be <u>not</u> a thought in thy wicked heart♥...KJV

- *Just imagine:*

    The book of Deuteronomy was written by Moses 1407 BC (Before Christ).

    (So much wisdom)

> Jesus spoke in <u>Mark 7:20-21</u> "...That which cometh out of the man, that defileth the man. ²¹ For from within, out of the heart♥ of men, proceed evil thoughts, adulteries, fornications, murders, ²² Thefts, covetousness, wickedness, deceit, lasciviousness, an evil eye, blasphemy, pride, foolishness: ²³ All these evil things come from within, and defile the man." KJV electronic ed.

- *Illumination from scripture provides daily revelations for transformation.*

<u>Hebrew 4:12</u> For the word of God is living and active and sharper than any two-edged sword, and piercing as far as the division of soul and spirit, of both joints and marrow, and able to judge the thoughts and intentions of the heart♥. NASB

- *At an early age, good, and bad habits become <u>imbedded</u> in the <u>sub</u>conscious mind. Many individuals unconsciously operate in automatic with no reflections or awareness of their behavior.*

<u>Isaiah 5:21</u> Woe unto them that are wise in their own eyes, and prudent in their own sight! KJV

Be humble, watch pride, ego, and arrogance.

Ego, pride, and arrogance = a false sense of security.

Evil rejects good.... evil cannot distinguish bad from good

NOTES

Wolf in Sheep's Clothing

NOTES

Woe to Those who are Wise in Their Own Eyes, and Clever in Their Own Sight!
Isaiah 5:21 NASB

The Wolf in Sheep Clothing

Deceitful

Disrupts

Jesus spoke in Matthew 7:15 "Beware of false prophets, which come to you in sheep's clothing, but inwardly they are ravening wolves. ¹⁶ Ye shall know them by their fruits." KJV

Eventually… confusion…than… total chaos..they try to confuse people

Psalm 82:5 "They know nothing, they understand nothing. They walk about in darkness; all the foundations of the earth are shaken. NIV

2 Timothy 4:3-4 For the time will come when men will not put up with sound doctrine. Instead, to suit their own desires, they will gather around them a great number of teachers to say what their itching ears want to hear. They turn their ears away from the truth and turn aside to myths. NIV

Jesus spoke in Matthew 15:18 "But those things which proceed out of the mouth come forth from the heart♥; and they defile the man. ¹⁹ For out of the heart♥ proceed evil thoughts, murders, adulteries, fornications, thefts, false witness, blasphemies." KJV

Misplaced emotions played out in life!

Get off the seesaw… Holding on to pre-conceived ideas might make us feel safe… But are we safe?

Isaiah 59:2+4 But your iniquities have separated between you and your God, and your sins have hid *his* face from you, that he will not hear. ⁴ None calleth for justice, nor *any* pleadeth for truth: they trust in vanity, and speak lies; they conceive mischief, and bring forth iniquity. KJV

Don't fall for the lies! There are people who can justify everything & anything!

And do not participate in the unfruitful deeds of darkness, but instead even expose them; for it is disgraceful even to speak of the things which are done by them in secret.
Ephesians 5:11-12 NASB

NOTES

Different Behavior-Personality Types

The following four (4) pages:

- *Aggressive Behavior*
- *Passive-Aggressive Behavior*
- *Assertive Behavior*
- *Controllers*
- *Satan….the devil*

NOTES

Aggressive Behavior

Understanding the Aggressive Personalities

http://counsellingresource.com/features/2008/11/03/aggressive-person

By Dr George Simon, PhD

"Aggressive personalities are fundamentally at war with anything that stands in the way of their unrestrained pursuit of their desires."

***

Passive-Aggressive Behavior

[The following article regarding a company's culture…this can be reflected on any organization or entity]

http://www.forbes.com/sites/amyanderson/2013/03/06/passive-aggressive-behavior-will-destroy-a-companys-culture

Passive-Aggressive Behavior Will Destroy a Company's Culture Amy Rees Anderson, Contributor

"I share my insights as an entrepreneur turned mentor & angel investor.

Passive-aggressive behavior in any company is one of the most destructive cancers to a culture that ends up killing both a great company, and the self-esteem of the individuals working there.

For any wondering what passive-aggressive behavior looks like, I will try and give some examples that paint a picture. A passive-aggressive person is someone who:

- on the surface appears to be agreeable and supportive, but behind the scenes will backstab, undercut, and sabotage.
- constantly states that you can trust their words when their actions have consistently shown that not to be true.

NOTES

Continued – <u>Passive-Aggressive Behavior</u>

- makes promises about things when they have no intention of ever following through, often then blaming things that were "out of their control" for precluding them from being able to fulfill their promise.
- smiles and agrees with you to your face, but then disagrees or even sabotages things behind your back.
- states "I was supportive of you, but this other person wasn't so there is nothing I can do" in order to place blame on someone else rather than voicing their own lack of support for the matter.
- gives positive praise and feedback to you directly, but then takes actions to undercut you to coworkers and management.
- withholds important information from other employees in order to make themselves appear more important and more valuable and in an attempt to make others around them fail.
- uses sarcasm or humor to make fun of someone else so they can hide behind an "I was just kidding" attitude, when really they meant every word.
- wants everyone to believe that they are their biggest supporter and advocate, refusing to be honest and direct with their true feelings.

Recently, I observed a company where passive-aggressive behavior is rapidly becoming embedded into the culture of the organization. The behavior appeared to initially stem from several members of <u>upper management</u>, and it quickly began to <u>permeate throughout all levels of the company</u>. As employees observed their coworkers getting rewarded for <u>passive-aggressive behavior</u>, they either took the "if you can't beat 'em, join 'em" road, or they began seeking employment opportunities elsewhere in order to escape the <u>toxic environment</u>. As the <u>toxic behavior spread,</u> employees started becoming depressed and despondent. What had once been a company that employees were excited to be a part of became nothing more than a paycheck they would collect until something better came along. Observing this cancer as it spread throughout the organization was unbelievably painful, especially as I watched the impact to those great individuals that were trying desperately to "hang in there" out of loyalty to their clients and loyalty to the business they once loved.

Good Leaders Are Invaluable To A Company. Bad Leaders Will Destroy It."

***

NOTES

<u>*Assertive Behavior*</u>

http://www.mayoclinic.com/health/assertive/SR00042

Being assertive: Reduce stress, communicate better. Assertiveness can help you control stress and anger and improve coping skills. Recognize and learn assertive behavior and communication. by Mayo Clinic staff

Being assertive is a core communication skill. Being assertive means that you express yourself effectively and stand up for your point of view, while also respecting the rights and beliefs of others. Being assertive can also help boost your self-esteem and earn others' respect. This can help with stress management, especially if you tend to take on too many responsibilities because you have a hard time saying no.

Some people seem to be naturally assertive. But if you're not one of them, you can learn to be more assertive.

Why assertive communication makes sense

Because assertiveness is based on mutual respect, it's an effective and diplomatic communication style. Being assertive shows that you respect yourself, because you're willing to stand up for your interests and express your thoughts and feelings.

It also demonstrates that you're aware of the rights of others and are willing to work on resolving conflicts.

Of course, it's not just what you say — your message — but also how you say it that's important. Assertive communication is direct and respectful. Being assertive gives you the best chance of successfully delivering your message. If you communicate in a way that's too passive or too aggressive, your message may get lost because people are too busy reacting to your delivery.

***

http://www.manipulative-people.com/aggressive-and-assertive-behavior

"Assertive behavior is a key element of healthy, independent, adult functioning. But because asserting oneself is a form of "fighting" for one's legitimate needs, it's easy to get confused about the difference between aggressive and assertive behavior." By Dr. Simon who wrote <u>*Character Disturbance.*</u>

NOTES

Controllers

The following is about aggressive and manipulative controllers, taken from Dr. Henry Cloud & Dr. John Townsend book:

"Boundaries: When to Say Yes, How to Say No to Take Control of Your Life" (page 54-55)

"1. Aggressive controllers: These people clearly don't listen to others' boundaries. They run over other people's fences like a tank. They are sometimes verbally abusive, sometimes physically abusive. But most of the time they simply aren't aware that others even have boundaries. It's as if they live in a world of yes. There's no place for someone else's no. They attempt to get others to change, to make the world fit their idea of the way life should be. They neglect their own responsibility to accept others as they are.

2. Manipulative controllers: Less honest than the aggressive controllers, manipulators try to persuade people out of their boundaries. They talk others into yes. They indirectly manipulate circumstances to get their own way. They seduce others into carrying their burdens. They use guilt messages."

Satan…..the devil

> Jesus spoke in Luke 11:17-18 "…Any kingdom divided against itself will be ruined, and a house divided against itself will fall. If Satan is divided against himself, how can his kingdom stand?" NIV
>
> Jesus spoke in John 10:10 "The thief comes only to steal, and kill, and destroy; I came that they might have life and might have it abundantly." NASB

Satan, the devil, is opposite of love. Satan loves decadence, lies, is deceitful, manipulative, tears down what is good and yes will murder. He sees life from scarcity and not God's abundance. His group will die with their lies.

With Jesus, search for truths, "The truth will set you free." But first surrender to Jesus and ask for forgiveness from the past, from those who have hurt you, and also forgiveness for yourself, and begin to see.

One can be free with God or dependent with Satan!

NOTES

What Fuels Your Engine???

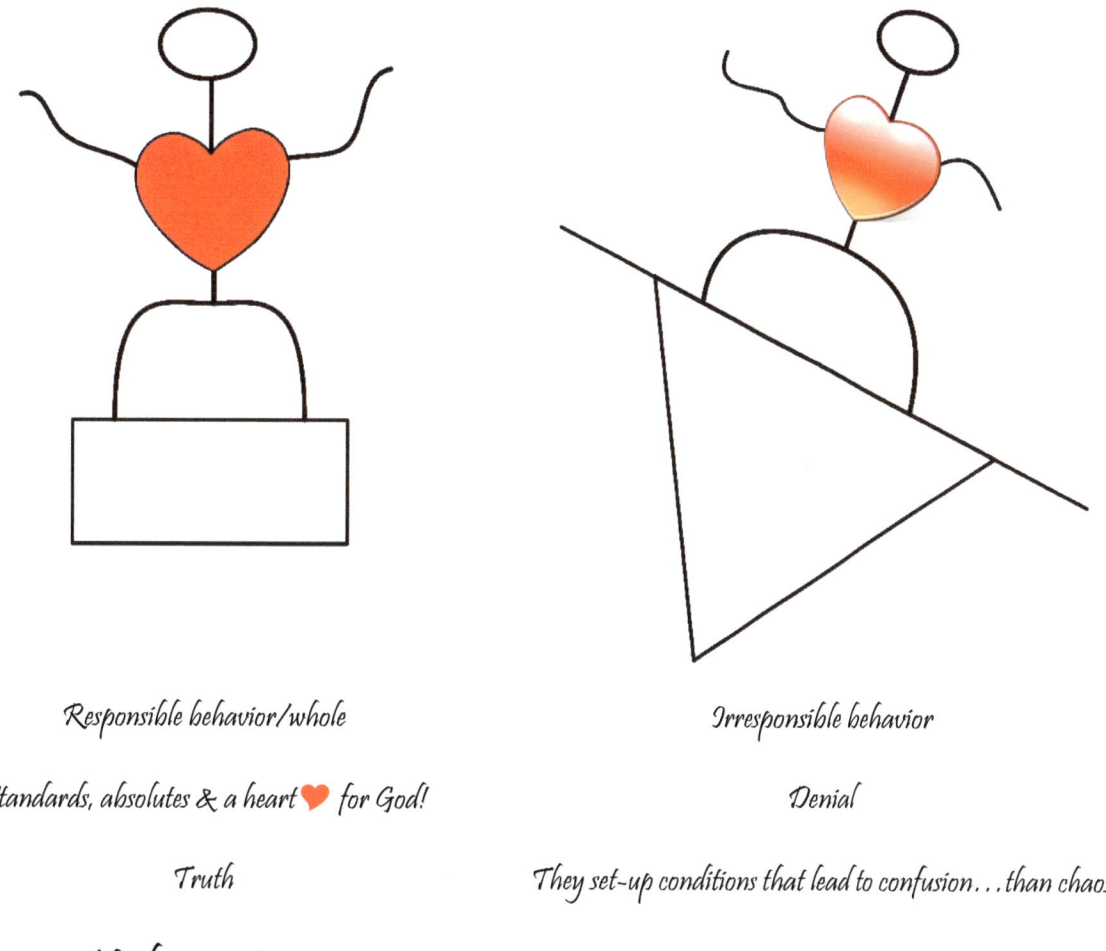

Responsible behavior/whole

Standards, absolutes & a heart ♥ for God!

Truth

Higher existence

Irresponsible behavior

Denial

They set-up conditions that lead to confusion...than chaos

Lower existence

I Corinthians 14:33 For God is not the author of confusion but of peace...KJV

Faith...surrender to Him...and break the cycle!

NOTES

A Fools Voice

Solomon, in 935 B.C., now older, reflects on past experiences from his life in the book of Ecclesiastes:

Ecclesiastes 5:1 Guard your steps as you go to the house of God, and draw near to listen rather than to offer the sacrifice of fools; for they do not know they are doing evil. NASB

Ecclesiastes 12:12 But beyond this, my son, be warned: the writing of many books is endless, and excessive devotion to books is wearying to the body. NASB

His wisdom is security ….. Stand in awe of God

- *Planting the word into one's heart & child's heart 24/7, water and nourish with love and enjoy God's Blessings and the fruits produced from hearing "His Word".*
- *Question to you: If a child watches murders on TV, violence, plays games with hate, anger, revenge, movies showing teens and adults jumping into bed, disrespect for parents & elders, pregnancy without marriage etc., what do you think are the percentages of the child building a solid foundation, being productive, and producing good fruits??? What will they hold in their hearts?? What will they pass down to the next generation??*

Zechariah 7:11-13 "But they refused to pay attention; stubbornly they turned their backs and stopped up their ears. They made their hearts ♥ as hard as flint and would not listen to the law or to the words that the Lord Almighty had sent by His Spirit through the earlier prophets. So the Lord Almighty was very angry." NIV

Ephesians 2:1 As for you, were dead in your transgressions and sins, in which you used to live when you followed the way of this world ….NIV

Think about it! Over 2,000 years ago they spoke of hardened hearts. ♥

NOTES

A Heart for God: He Will Awaken Your True Hidden Self

- *2,000 years later and tons of information available, how many experts speak on the dangers of a harden heart and evil thoughts?*
- *The Bible teaches principles, setting boundaries, truth, and goodness.*

    Lessons are learned about the importance of the condition of the heart and the thoughts we hold in our head…which affect our behavior..Then there are the consequences.

With the Word of God, the Bible, the Great Textbook holds all wisdom. With wisdom and a heart for God, discernment will help give you and give children insights on how to use the knowledge that was acquired through a heart♥ that knows God.

- *Thoughts (belief system) = the results = good or bad consequences!*

> Jesus spoke in <u>John 14:12</u> "Verily, verily, I say unto you, He that believeth on me, the works that I do shall he do also; and greater *works* than these shall he do; because I go unto my Father. ¹³ And whatsoever ye shall ask in my name, that will I do, that the Father may be glorified in the Son." KJV

The Word = fruits of the Spirit

The Word = thoughts = the Fruits of the Spirit

A heart♥ created from the Word of God!

<u>Roman 12:2</u> And be not conformed to this world: but be ye transformed by the renewing of your mind. KJV

> Jesus spoke in <u>Mark 1:14</u> ... Jesus came into Galilee, preaching the gospel of the kingdom of God, ¹⁵ And saying, "The time is fulfilled, and the kingdom of God is at hand: repent ye, and believe the gospel." KJV

<u>Romans 8:31</u> If God be for us, who can be against us? KJV

With Faith→surrender to Him→and break the cycle→search for truths!

NOTES

The Nature of God & God's Nature

- Jesus teaches us about the loving nature of God by learning about the character of Jesus.
- By trusting in Jesus, you will begin to see God's nature. Jesus is Love and Peace! God objects to evil and to go against God's love nature is <u>un-natural</u>. God does <u>not</u> like evil; it is <u>against God's nature</u>.

<u>Why some people cannot see what is in front of them?</u>

1. Preconceived ideas: Fox p. 6, "It seems that human nature is very prone to believe what it wants to believe, rather than to incur the labor of really searching the scriptures with an open mind."
2. Judging without comparing ideas and the facts
3. Too busy justifying their position and intentions (anything can be justified!)
4. The blame game
5. Misplaced (unresolved emotions; pain, anger, jealousy etc.)
6. Some possessive preconceived ideas have been made concrete in stone early as 5 or 10 years. Decisions made on how one saw the world, how one perceived people, situations etc. A preconceived idea could have occurred based out of fear, hate, rage, hurt, pain etc.
7. Etc..

I am not here to beat up on you; but to give food for thought and growth. God will guide, with peace, those whose hearts ♥ are open and willing.

There are laws established in nature. When we do go against God's loving nature, there will be natural consequences.

$$Cause \longrightarrow Effect \longrightarrow Consequence$$

<u>Psalm 82:5</u> They know not, neither will they understand; they walk on in darkness: all the foundations of the earth are out of course. KJV

Out of course, out of sync, does not flow with the nature of God. If evil is against God's nature and boundaries are ignored, the consequence could be devastating. Evil spreads…..Similar to one rotten apple in a basket of good apples. When I was a kid, I had to wrap up each apple in paper, so when one apple rotted, it did not touch and rot the other apples.

<u>Isaiah 30:18</u> for the Lord is a God of judgment: blessed are all they that wait for Him. KJV

NOTES

The Gospel, the Good News!

Jesus left a part of Him with us, the Spirit of Life, the Holy Spirit to empower each one of us. He does intervene. Invite Him in to dwell in your heart ♥ and be inspired by walking <u>in-spirit</u>.

♥

When we wholeheartedly believe, a new life will begin to enfold and this new life continues on eternally. He continually provides our needs each day. Each person is unique, an individual, God wants to set us free, He makes us whole, and fill's that empty void.

Noah Webster's 1828 Dictionary…Whole - Fear

<u>Whole</u> – The entire thing; the entire of total assemblage of parts. The whole of religion is contained in the short precept "Love God with all your heart ♥, and your neighbor as yourself. Fear God and keep His commandments, for this is the whole duty of man. <u>Ecclesiastes xii</u>.

Jesus spoke in <u>Mark 5:8</u> For Jesus had said to him, "Come out of this man, you evil spirit!" NIV

Jesus spoke in <u>Mark 5:34</u> "Daughter, they faith hath made thee whole; go in peace." KJV

Noah Webster's 1828

<u>Fear</u> – (2) to reverence; to have a reverential awe;

Jesus, our teacher, sacrificed His life for all our sins. He was the sacrificial lamb for the sins of God's children. He sacrificed and died to release us from the bondage of sin and guilt. By His teachings and by His Blessings and Graces, there is hope, truth, justice, and mercy.

Praise be to You, Lord Jesus Christ!

NOTES

Un-forgiveness

Un-forgiveness is bondage, a stronghold, a foothold. Not being able to recognize or sort out our feelings can be an obstacle which can set us back for years. The pains from the past, the roots of anger, resentments, hurt, guilty conscience etc., without forgiveness, can keep us in bondage. With unresolved past emotions there is unrest. Without forgiveness, one might see life situations through a distorted lens. Believing in Christ, asking Him to help us in forgiving others, forgiving ourselves, we begin to come out of darkness and into the light.

John 1:10-14 He was in the world, and the world was made through Him, and the world did not know Him. He came to His own, and those who were His own did not receive Him. But as many as received Him, to them He gave the right to become children of God, even to those who believe in His name, who were born not of blood, nor of the will of the flesh, nor of the will of man, but of God. And the Word became flesh, and dwelt among us, and we beheld His glory, glory as of the only begotten from the Father, full of grace and truth. NASB

"The Word" is Alive!

Forgive others, forgive yourself, and release the guilt that is held because of sin. Give it to God and forgive, even if it takes 70 x 7.

> Jesus spoke in Matthew 18:21-22 Then Peter came and said to Him, "Lord, how often shall my brother sin against me and I forgive him? Up to seven times?" Jesus said to him, "I do not say to you up to seven times, but up to seventy times seven." KJV

Forgive those in the past and present, and change your future with Him:

- Eternal life
- Emotional healing
- Forgiving generational sins that have been past down from one generation to the next
- Break the cycle
- Change the course

NOTES

Glory to God!

> Jesus spoke in <u>Matthew 6:21</u> "For where your treasure is, there your heart♥ will be also."
>
> Jesus spoke in <u>Matthew 6:33</u> "But seek ye first the kingdom of God, and his righteousness; and all these things shall be added unto you."
>
> Jesus spoke in <u>Matthew 9:22</u> But Jesus turned him about, and when he saw her, he said, "Daughter, be of good comfort; thy faith hath made thee whole."
>
> Jesus spoke in <u>Matthew 12:35</u> "A good man out of the good treasure of the heart♥ bringeth forth good things: and an evil man out of the evil treasure bringeth forth evil things. But I say unto you, that every idle word that men shall speak, they shall give account thereof in the day of judgment."
>
> Jesus spoke in <u>John 14:15</u> "If ye love me, keep my commandments. And I will pray the Father, and he shall give you another Comforter, that he may abide with you for ever; *Even* the Spirit of truth; whom the world cannot receive, because it seeth him not, neither knoweth him: but ye know him; for he dwelleth with you, and shall be in you."

All above verses from King James Bible

<u>I John 1:8-9</u> If we say that we have no sin, we are deceiving ourselves, and the truth is not in us. If we confess our sins, He is faithful and righteous to forgive us our sins and to cleanse us from all unrighteousness. NASB

- *The Spirit, His Spirit is within me. He is preparing me & will guide me because He is the way, He is the truth, and He is life. Do not be troubled. God's plan is at work. Progress is in the process. Dig deep, study, research, and reflect on the truth.*

<u>Ephesians 3:14-21</u> For this reason I bow my knees before the Father, from whom every family in heaven and on earth derives its name, that He would grant you, according to the riches of His glory, to be strengthened with power through His Spirit in the inner man; so that Christ may dwell in your hearts♥ through faith; and that you, being rooted and grounded in love, may be able to comprehend with all saints what is the breadth and length and height and depth, and to know the love of Christ which surpasses knowledge, that you may be filled up all the fullness of God. Now to Him who is able to do exceeding abundantly beyond all that we ask or think, according to the **power that works within us**, to Him be the glory in the church and in Christ Jesus to all generations forever and ever. Amen. NASB

NOTES

++Jesus++ Son of God++

Matthew 1:21 She will give birth to a Son, and you are to give Him the name Jesus, because He will save His people from their sins. NIV

> Jesus spoke in John 4:34-35 "My food," said Jesus, "is to do the will of Him who sent me and to finish His work. Do you not say, "Four months more and then the harvest"? I tell you, open your eyes and look at the fields! They are ripe for harvest. Even now the reaper draws his wages, even now he harvest the crop for eternal life, so that the sower and the reaper may be glad together. Thus the saying "One sows and another reaps' is true. I sent you to reap what you have not worked for. Others have done the hard work, and you have reaped the benefits of their labor." NIV

With faith, believing in Jesus, he refines us and we grow reflecting on His Word. It might not look like the way I would put the pieces together; but when He finishes, it is better than my imagination.

> Jesus spoke in John 6:40 "For this is the will of My Father, that everyone who beholds the Son and believes in Him, may have eternal life; and I Myself will raise him up on the last day." NASB

Philippians 4:13 I can do all things through Christ which strengthens me. KJV

He enables me and I grow and advance a little every day. I can see the difference 20 years ago, 10 years ago and the pattern of my life and where I was headed....not good! Am I perfect? Far from it. The only perfect one is The Lord who created us. And we are very fortunate that He wants to share His wisdom with us.

Titus 3:3-7 At one time we to were foolish, disobedient, deceived and enslaved by all kinds of passions and pleasures. We lived in malice and envy, being hated and hating one another. But when the kindness and love of God our Savior appeared, He saved us, not because of righteous things we had done, but because of His mercy. He saved us through the washing or rebirth and renewal by the Holy Spirit, whom He poured out on us generously through Jesus Christ our Savior, so that, having been justified by His grace, we might become heirs having the hope of eternal life. NIV

Colossians 2:2-3+9-10 that their hearts ♥ may be encouraged, having been knit together in love, and attaining to all the wealth that comes from the full assurance of understanding, resulting in a true knowledge of God's mystery, that is, Christ Himself, in whom are hidden all the treasures of wisdom and knowledge. For in Him all the fullness of Deity dwells in bodily form, and in Him you have been made complete, and He is the head over all rule and authority... NASB

Hebrew 1:3 And He is the radiance of His glory and the exact representation of His nature, and upholds all things by the word of His power. When He had made purification of sins, He sat down at the right hand of the Majesty on high; ....NASB

NOTES

++++ *Jesus* ++++

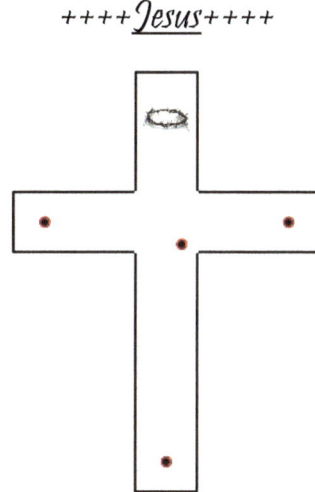

Jesus spoke in Luke 23:24 "Forgive them Father, for they do not know what they do!" KJV

In the Old Testament, people sacrificed a lamb in repentance of their sins. They were familiar with the meaning of sacrificial lamb. Jesus the sacrificial lamb for all sinners, the people at that time understood the true meaning of Jesus death.

The following is Isaiah predicting the death of Christ 700 years BC (Before the Birth of Christ):

Isaiah 53:5-6 But He was pierced for our transgressions, He was crushed for our iniquities; the punishment that brought us peace was upon Him, and by His wounds we are healed. We all like sheep, have gone astray, each of us has turned to his own way; and the Lord has laid on Him the iniquity of us all. NIV

Ephesians 1:7-9 In Him we have redemption through His blood, the forgiveness of our trespasses, according to the riches of His grace, which He lavished upon us. In all wisdom and insight He made known to us the mystery of His will…..NASB

1 John:1:8-10 If we say that we have no sin, we are deceiving ourselves, and the truth is not in us. If we confess our sins, He is faithful and righteous to forgive us our sins and to cleanse us from all unrighteousness. If we say that we have not sinned, we make Him a liar, and His word is not in us. NASB

Jesus spoke in Matthew 18:3-6 "…Truly I say to you, unless you are converted and become like children, you shall not enter the kingdom of heaven. Whoever than humbles himself as this child, he is the greatest in the kingdom of heaven. And whoever receives one such child in My name receives Me; but whoever causes one of these little ones who believe in Me to stumble, it is better for him that a heavy millstone be hung around his neck, and that he be drowned in the depth of the sea." NASB

NOTES

Jesus Loves You!

- *Jesus comes to restore peace*
- *Jesus comes to restore justice*
- *Jesus comes to share His Joy, His Blessings, and His Graces*
- *Jesus shows the road to prosperity by producing quality, value; and with His help this prosperity is built on a foundation that continuously gets stronger*
- *Jesus shares the character of God, His beauty, His goodness, and His Righteousness with us*
- *He breaks unhealthy patterns*
- *It is a process, like playing an instrument or starting a business. With Him, there is continual progress and growth*

Romans 5:1-2 Therefore, since we have been justified through faith, we have peace with God through our Lord Jesus Christ, through whom we have gained access by faith into this grace in which we now stand. And we rejoice in the hope of the glory of God. NIV

> Jesus spoke in Matthew 19:4-6 "Have you not read, that He who created them from the beginning MADE THEM MALE AND FEMALE, and said, "FOR THIS CAUSE A MAN SHALL LEAVE HIS FATHER AND MOTHER, AND SHALL CLEAVE TO HIS WIFE; AND THE TWO SHALL BECOME ONE FLESH?" "Consequently they are no longer two, but one flesh. What therefore God has joined together let no man separate." NASB

I Corinthians 2:16 For WHO HAS KNOWN THE MIND OF THE LORD, THAT HE SHOULD INSTRUCT HIM? But we have the mind of Christ. NASB

Ephesians 2:5-10 Have this attitude in yourselves which was also in Christ Jesus, who, although He existed in the form of God, did not regard equality with God a thing to be grasped, but emptied Himself taking the form of a bond-servant, and being found in appearance as a man, He humbled Himself by becoming obedient to the point of death, even death on a cross. Therefore also God highly exalted Him, and bestowed on Him the name which is above every name, that at the name of Jesus EVERY KNEE SHOULD BOW, of those who are in heaven, and on earth, and under the earth…NASB

NOTES

Learn History............His Story

John 1:4 In Him was life, and life was the light of men.

I Corinthians 2:16 For WHO HAS KNOWN THE MIND OF THE LORD, THAT HE SHOULD INSTRUCT HIM? But we have the mind of Christ. NASB

Philippians 2:6 Who, being in very nature God, did not consider equality with God something to be grasped, but made himself nothing, taking the very nature of a servant, being made in human likeness. And being found in appearance as a man, he humbled himself and became obedient to death-even death on a cross. NIV

> Jesus spoke in John 3:21 "But whoever lives by the truth comes into the light, so that it may be seen plainly that what he has done has been done through God." NIV
>
> Jesus spoke in John 8:12 When Jesus spoke again to the people, He said, "I am the light of the world. Whoever follows me will never walk in darkness, but will have the light of life." NIV

2 Corinthians 4:4 The god of this age has blinded the minds of unbelievers, so that they cannot see the light of the gospel of the glory of Christ, who is the image of God. NIV

Romans 6:23 For the wages of sin is death, but the gift of God is eternal life in Christ Jesus our Lord. NIV

> Jesus spoke in John 15:3-5 "You are already clean because of the Word which I have spoken to you. Abide in Me, and I in you. As the branch cannot bear fruit of itself, unless it abides in the vine, so neither can you, unless you abide in Me. I am the vine, you are the branches; he who abides in Me, and I in him, he bears much fruit; for apart from Me you can do nothing." NASB

Ephesians 4:17-27 This I say therefore, and affirm together with the Lord, that you walk no longer just as the Gentiles also walk, in the futility of their mind, being darkened in their understanding, excluded from the life of God, because of the ignorance that is in them, because of the hardness of their heart ♥; and they, having become callous, have given themselves over to sensuality, for the practice of every kind of impurity with greediness. But you did not learn Christ in this way, if indeed you have heard Him and have been taught in Him, just as truth is in Jesus, that, in reference to your former manner of life you lay aside the old self, which is being corrupted in accordance with the lusts of deceit, and that you be renewed in the spirit of your mind, and put on the new self which in the likeness of God has been created in righteousness and holiness of the truth. Therefore, laying aside falsehood, speak TRUTH, each one of you, with his neighbor, for we are members of one another. NASB

Learn the character of Jesus, His life, death, and resurrection for our sins and for eternal life in Heaven with our Father, our creator. By following Jesus, He brings us a taste of Heaven on earth. Through Him, knowing Him, we will learn of God's love that is stored for each one of us. He gave each person freedom to choose life with Him or death with other gods.

NOTES

Renewal

Noah Webster's 1928 Dictionary... Spirit

Spirit - "Spirit is a substance in which thinking, knowing, doubting, and a power of moving do subsist" Locke.

> Jesus spoke in John 4:24+26-27 "God is spirit, and those who worship Him must worship in spirit and truth. But the Helper, the Holy Spirit, whom the Father will send in My name, He will teach you all things, and bring to your remembrance all that I said to you. Peace I leave with you; My peace I give to you; not as the world gives...." NASB
>
> Jesus spoke in John 15:24 "He who does not love Me does not keep My words;" NASB

Galatians 3:22 fruit of the Spirit is love, joy, peace, patience, kindness, goodness, faithfulness, gentleness, and self control.

- *The promises of freedom are given through the Love of God. Study the life of Moses and he speaks of individual freedoms. He spoke of individual freedoms between 1450-1410 BC (Before the birth of Christ). The Holy Spirit helps us release the bondages that keep us stuck. This freedom comes from faith in believing in Jesus Christ. The Holy Spirit will inspire you. He creates through those who have a heart ♥ for God!*

Philippians 4:4 Rejoice in the Lord always: *and* again I say, Rejoice. ⁵ Let your moderation be known unto all men. The Lord *is* at hand. ⁶ Be careful for nothing; but in everything by prayer and supplication with thanksgiving let your requests be made known unto God. ⁷ And the peace of God, which passeth all understanding, shall keep your hearts ♥ and minds through Christ Jesus. KJV

Galatians 5:24 Those who belong to Christ Jesus have crucified the sinful nature with its passions and desires. Since we live by the Spirit, let us keep in step with the Spirit. Let us not become conceited, provoking and envying each other. NIV

Acts 2:38 And Peter said to them, "Repent, and let each of you be baptized in the name of Jesus Christ for the forgiveness of your sins; and you shall receive the gift of the Holy Spirit." NASB

I Corinthians 12:13 For by one Spirit we were all baptized into one body, whether Jews or Greeks, whether slaves or free, and we were all made to drink on one Spirit. NASB

Ephesians 1:3 In Him, you also, after listening to the message of truth, the gospel of your salvation – having also believed, you were sealed in Him with the Holy Spirit of promise...NASB

NOTES

The Holy Bible

Emmett Fox wrote:

"The Bible teaches new ways of thinking and working, a continual revelation, it reveals, refreshes, moves me to the next step, the next level." P.29

- *Scripture verses are lessons and stories set up to make us reflect and think about the messages that God wants us to know and apply. He develops, uncovers, to "enlighten our thoughts", to think deeper, getting us out of the box thinking, to grow everyday by reflecting on His word for guidance. In Bible Study Fellowship (BSF), I learned a huge lesson. Sitting in a circle with a group of people, each person shared how one scripture verse had touched their lives and what they received from it. The same verse had touched and helped each person in different ways. We all have different events going on in our life and we are all unique; miraculously, the Bible is divinely written in a way to speak to each person individually. The Bible produces individual thinkers versus the collective mind.*

The disciple John records his reflections on Jesus (The Light) and John the Baptist:

John 1:6 There was a man sent from God, whose name *was* John (John the Baptist). 7 The same came for a witness, to bear witness of the Light, that all *men* through him might believe. 8 He was not that Light, but *was sent* to bear witness of that Light. 9 *That* was the true Light, which lighteth every man that cometh into the world. KJV

One way children learn and grow is from the many Bible stories of people's successes and failures. Parents and children gain wisdom and discernment by cross referencing the Bible, concordance, and Noah Webster's 1828 Dictionary. With prayers and journaling, writing in your own words how God enlightens with numerous valuable lessons, principles and insights. The stories that Christ gave to His people were stories (parables) to learn from, stories to be remembered. Two thousand years ago, the majority of people did not read or write. Their ear was sensitive to learning. Modern day stimulation and distractions such as television, computer games, etc. could be a hindrance to internal growth. The student of God will learn and be inspired from wise leaders, stories about people's weaknesses and strengths and how they overcame hurdles in their lives. God is truly Love! A Loving Father who wants the best for each one of you. He will bring out your strengths and talents and give guidance on the many different means to using your God given gifts!

Luke 24:27 And beginning with Moses and with all the prophets. He explained to them the things concerning Himself in all the Scriptures. NASB

2 Timothy 3:16-17 All Scripture is inspired by God and profitable for teaching, for reproof, for correction, for training in righteousness; that the man of God may be adequate, equipped for every good work. NASB

NOTES

The Great Textbook "The Holy Bible"

Philippians 2:13 for it is God who works in you to will and to act according to His good purpose. NIV

> Jesus spoke in Luke 24:45-47 Then He opened their minds so they could understand the Scriptures. He told them, "This is what is written: The Christ will suffer and rise from the dead on the third day, and repentance and forgiveness of sins will be preached in His name to all nations, beginning at Jerusalem." NIV
>
> Jesus spoke in John 7:38-39 "Whoever believes in me, as the Scripture has said, streams of living water will flow from within him." By this He meant the Spirit, whom those who believed in Him were later to receive……NIV

Colossians 1:5-6 ….the faith you have already heard about in the word of truth, the gospel that has come to you. All over the world this gospel is bearing fruit and growing, just as it has been doing among you since the day you heard it and understood God's grace in all its truth. NIV

1Timonthy 8:10 We know that the law is good if one uses it properly. We also know that law made not for the righteous but for lawbreakers and rebels, the ungodly and sinful, the unholy and irreligious; for those who kill their father or mothers, for murderers, for adulterers and perverts, for slave traders and liars and perjurers-and for whatever else is contrary to the sound doctrine. NIV

2 Peter 1:20-21 Above all, you must understand that no prophesy of Scripture came about by the prophet's own interpretation. For prophecy never had its origin in the will of man, but men spoke from God as they were carried along by the Holy Spirit. NIV

Hebrews 4:12:13 For the Word of God is living and active. Sharper than any double-edged sword, it penetrates even to dividing soul and spirit, joints and marrow; it judges the thoughts and attitudes of the heart♥. Nothing in all creation is hidden from God's sight. Everything is uncovered and laid bare before the eyes of Him to whom we must give account.NIV

NOTES

Cliffhangers

For years I attended many different types of seminars. Think about the following true events and come up with your own scenarios of how the stories could have affected a person's entire life: come from cause, effect, and consequence:

- A young child was always called stupid. One day in the third grade the child said "I am going to do it; I am going to study every day after school and on weekends to prove myself." So for one year that child did exactly that and on the last report card of that year, the child received most 100% except for one grade in the 90%. The child ran home to show the father. "Look what I did" and handed the report card to the father. The child applied his best efforts and stood tall and smiling proud for attaining the goal. His father took a look at the report card, threw the report card to the child and said, "Is this the best you could do kid?"

    <u>Question</u>: How do you think the child felt? How do you think this affected his future performances? When the father called the child kid, was this respectful?

- A fifth grader and sixth grader stirred up trouble and tried to get other kids in school to get a teacher fired. They were both sent into the principal's office, each to tell their story. After conference with the school principle, the fifth grader said to his friend the sixth grader "you were lying; I did not say that, it was your idea." The sixth grader said, "If I go down, you are going down with me!" <u>Question</u>: What do you think the foundation and the pattern of their life was and where do you think it might end up for each if they did not learn from this lesson?

- A very young child was left with a babysitter every day while the parents went to work. The sitter dressed that young boy as a girl with a dress and a little purse and did girly things. <u>Question</u>: What do you think the sitter's behavior had on this young child's mind and emotion?   What affect could have been a result of the sitter's action day in and day out?

- A six year old boy was having dinner with mother, father, and sister. The father left the table to go to his bedroom. The family heard a shot and the father shot himself in the head. The young boy was crying and someone said "Shh……big boys don't cry." <u>Question</u>: Did anyone ever have time to help him deal with grief, and possibly guilt etc…?? The boy now 55 years old, walks in anger and does not even realize it. What unresolved emotions can he be carrying upon his heart ❤ ?

NOTES

Part 2 of Cliffhangers

- A father wanted a little boy and had many daughters. The father called the youngest daughter "boy" and never by her real name. Dad "I'm a girl."
  <u>Question:</u> What do you thing could have been the results as she got older....?

- A minister and his family frequently moved from one town to the next. Finally, they settled for about three years in one town. His son now sixteen was so happy; he was in a school where he made many friends. Then his father announced that the family was moving and relocating out of state. The son reacted and made an announcement to his minister father to embarrass him and stick it to him, "And now I found myself.........?" People do strange things out of anger. The mind is very powerful; we can talk ourselves into anything.

- A little boy of five years old was acting very strange and distant for two weeks. The mother did not know what to do...she felt the pain that he was feeling. She finally asked him, "Is there something that is bothering you? Can I help? The son said, "I know that you don't want me!" Those words were like a dagger through the mother's heart ♥. The mother asked "Why do you say that?" The son said "Because you told Mrs. T that "you did not want me"! The son overheard a conversation that his mother & father were not planning on having children because they were in their 30's and had careers, were spoiled and set in their ways. The son, from the conversation believed the mother did not want him. To reinforce her love to her beautiful and loving son, the mother kept telling her son that she was surprised that she was going to have a baby. That he was a gift from God; and she told him the wonderful story of his birth. "When he was born, they placed him on her chest. She saw how beautiful he was. That he had beautiful tan skin, it appeared that one strand of hair was brown and another blond, that his cheeks were chubby and so cute that the nurses just wanted to squeeze them, and that the nurses called him "rose-bud lips" because he has the most beautiful lips! The mother told him she was so happy that God put him in her life....She did not know that she had so much love inside of her. So much love, because of him...her beautiful little boy! "Many times afterwards, he would ask his mother to repeat the story of his birth.
  <u>Question:</u> What do you think could have happened to this young boy if his mother did not ask him or never was able to figure out what was affecting his mood and behavior?

NOTES

Part 3 of *Cliffhanger*

- *This is a simple example and form of pattern passed down from one generation to the next:*

    A woman was preparing a roast for dinner. A friend asked her why she cuts her roast in-half to cook it. She has been cutting the roast in two pieces for ten years just like her mother always prepared it. She asked her mother, and her mother said, "That in her early marriage, she had a tiny apartment, stove, and oven that were half the size of a stove that we have today. The roast was cut in two pieces to be able to fit the pan that fit the oven." Well, the point is; behavior patterns (good & bad) could be passed down from one generation to the next.

- *One of the stories from the Bible I want to share is from Genesis and the story of Adam and Eve. When God created Adam and Eve, He had them living in Paradise, where there was plenty of food, no death, everything was perfect....heaven on earth. God gave Adam and Eve one commandment; they can eat from any tree freely, but not from the tree of the knowledge of good and evil, for in that day <u>they would surely die.</u> But the serpent enticed Eve to eat from the forbidden tree and gave also to her husband, and he ate; afterwards, they realized that they were naked and covered themselves. Their lives were separated from God.*

    - <u>Genesis 3:8-13 NIV</u> Then the man and his wife heard the sound of the Lord God as He was walking in the garden in the cool of the day, and they hid from the Lord God among the trees of the garden. But the Lord God called to the man, "Where are you?" He (Adam) answered, "I heard you in the garden, and I was afraid because I was naked, so I hid." And He said, "Who told you that you were naked? Have you eaten from the tree that I commanded you not to eat from?" The man said, "The woman you put here with me—she gave me some fruit from the tree, and I ate it." Then the Lord God said to the woman, "What is this you have done?" The woman said, "The serpent deceived me, and I ate."

    When God called to Adam and Eve, they hid, avoided to answer directly on their misbehavior and tried to cover—up their sins, did the blame game ...sound familiar?? Jesus came to give life through His Spirit, to work internally in each one of us.

- *A young girl was raped by her father, uncles, and brothers from a very early age and through her teen years. What effect do you think this had on her behavior and how do you see her future life with forgiveness and without forgiveness.*

I pray, for all those who have been hurt, to see God's love, and His Spirit indwell in each heart ♥ *with His saving Graces.*

He helps break those patterns in our life that do not serve us well today. God is of peace and not evil...Our Heavenly Father wants to see the best for us. With faith, believing in His Word, He will help us each day through tough times. There is enlightenment working in us with the Comforters' help, for today, tomorrow, and eternity!   Thanks be to God!

NOTES

Challenges

Do any of the following topics interest you? Have fun researching and using the Holy Bible, Concordance, and Noah Webster's 1828 Dictionary. <u>Suggestion:</u> Carry a small 3x5" notebook and every idea from books, radio, speaking to people and when that light bulb goes off in your head write it down. I have two gallon size plastic bags filled with notebooks and the theme that kept repeating was on man's foundation. That is how I started with my research and then began writing. Try researching with a buddy or a group of your friends. Or after seeing a movie, discuss with friends the characters in the movie, and their behavior etc. It could be a lot of fun and educational.

God Bless you and all you do!

<u>Suggested Topics:</u>

- If a statement contains truth and half-truths, does this make it a true statement?
- What does the meaning of the Cross mean to you?
- What is the difference between passive, assertive, aggressive behavior? How does this relate to boundaries? For yourself and/or in respect to another person's boundaries?
- There are different types of agreements. Using Noah Webster's 1828 Dictionary, define the following: covenant, contracts, agreement, promises, intentions, written and verbal contracts etc. Can you find stories in the Bible mentioning the above?
- Who are the people in the Old Testament or New Testament that lived their life with God's abundant graces and blessings?
- Who is Satan, demons, devil, anti-Christ and in what forms?
- What is unconditional and conditional love?
- What does accountable and being responsible mean to you? <u>Suggestion:</u> Journal your thoughts on this subject before and after your research. See the growth!
- What does sin mean to you and the results from sin? And how could it affect the people around you?

NOTES

Part 2 of <u>Challenges</u>

- What are some things that could be passed down from one generation to the next? <u>Suggestions:</u> Interviewing people on their responses to this question.
- How can we help the weak get stronger? What are the many different ways that people are weak, strong and what does God say about this?
- Who in the Bible had an abundant mindset, creative productive mind? Who had a mindset that came from scarcity and taking from others?
- What does personal responsibility mean to you? Self-governing?
- What does the conscious mind and subconscious mind mean to you? Your thoughts before your research and afterward.
- What are the names of Jesus and what do they mean to you? Example: Light, Counselor, Bread of Life, Chief Shepherd, Cornerstone, Dayspring, Good Shepherd, Great High Priest
- What does the Bible say about the role of a leader?
- What breaks relationships with God?
- Why should we admit our mistakes?
- Who in the Bible had a relationship with God and without God?
- Who was transformed after knowing and learning of God, Jesus, and His Word? Tell your personal story and record people's testimonies how Jesus helped them personally.
- What is the difference between love and lust and which one is long lasting? And why?
- What does it say about murder in the Bible? Types of murder?
- Tell the story of Joseph and his relationship with his brothers who sold him into slavery…in Genesis chapter 37:1 to chapter 50:26. Where did Joseph's faith in God take him?
- What does individual freedom mean to you vs. the collective mind?
- Christ wants unity, Satan wants division, Satan pits one person after the other, and Christ wants us to build relationship. What does the Bible say about both?
- In building strong character traits, is it sometimes easier for children than adults and why?
- What is the church, who is the head of the church, what is the purpose of the church?
- How do we overcome division and should unity be forced?

NOTES

Part 3 of <u>Challenges</u>

- *Do you think God wants us to fight for righteousness…or do you think He wants us to fight to win? What is the difference? What about the conscience in each scenario?*
- *What is the Tower of Babel? Why was it built? Why did God not like it?*
- *If each person is sacred to God and we are created in His image…What separates us from Him? Why?*
- *Many people have fallen for the lie, that they are not good enough, not enough talent. We each have talents and gifts, strengths that God has given us… Why do you think people fall (believe) in false lies? About their own gifts and talents? How does God build up our talents, gifts, strengths?*
- *In Genesis 9:17 … Be fruitful and fill the earth…… What do you think God meant by this statement?*
- *God has and will accomplish "His Will" through imperfect people. List some of those imperfect people in the Bible and how His message, the Gospel of Good News, moved the "Word of God" from the east to the west.*
- *What gives birth to the agents of the antichrist?*

NOTES

Questions to Ponder and Answer for your journal

What are your views on the following topics?

God

How do you picture God?

What do you know about the Bible?

What do you think is a weak and strong foundation?

What is Love?

Peace of Mind? Do you have peace?

Justice - What does this mean to you?

Truth - What is truth?

Holy Spirit - Have you experienced the power of the Holy Spirit?

What part of life is growth to you?

What is maturity?

After finishing answering the questions, compare your answers from day one when you began to journal.

What were your thoughts and compare?

NOTES

Final

Moral pollution to the environment is against God's nature and also blinding. Evil is against God's loving nature. He provides unity through salvation in Christ. The most important commandment is love in Matthew 22:37-39. When we are against His loving nature, there are natural consequences in nature that He set in place. Remember cause, effect, consequence? It not only affects one person, it could affect others, relationships, family, as well as, affecting the nation and the world……. Does it go against God's nature?

You have to want to change, improve, and develop by admitting and being honest with yourself first and praying to God to heal all wounds. Remember, if we fall for the lies, than we are blinded from seeing truths. Admitting and being honest with ourselves, with forgiveness, begins the process of closing that open wound. <u>Seal</u> the wound with the <u>Holy Spirit</u> in prayer. The process of healing is with believing and surrendering to Jesus in prayer.

Lean on Him to fulfill your full potential. He provides great gifts to each of us in this wonderful gift of life. This gift of life from God, our Creator, grows in amazing ways. He takes those weaknesses and turns them into strengths in a strange and wonderful way. Paul knew his weaknesses and relied on God for His strength, "so that Christ power may rest on me." (2Corinthians 12:9 NIV) Moses also knew his weakness and leaned on God. Walk with Christ and He will be your Guide! In Luke 19:11 (NIV footnote), Jesus expects us to use these talents so that they can multiply and the Kingdom grows.

With His Word, there is renewal, building, transformation. He deals with all; we just have to give our hearts ❤ to Him for this fulfillment of life and love and into eternity with Him!

Whatever you do, be the best you can be, and give it your best shot. If you're just starting out and have to take a minimum wage job, than learn and grow where you are. You will learn people skills, responsibility, operation of a business, maybe teach, managing or writing a book. During your job interview, you will agree to terms with the employer or manager. Stick with the terms and create value by producing quality work in whatever you do. Someday, if your goal is to own your own business, remember; to be a good employer, you need to be a good employee. Pay attention to the details. Business owners take a big risk starting and running a business. They have to know many areas in the operation of the business; and many times it is on the job training. Support and be a good employee. When employees behavior shortchange s(sabotage) the boss and company, the employee also shortchanges, cheats, or sabotages themselves with this scarcity mentality. This sabotage scarcity mentality will keep a person from advancing in their growth and career.

With "The Word of God", there is encouragement and support in cultivating, developing, and in nurturing you through the steps. With Him, one step at a time, there is a new life with new ways, growing, advancing and improving with the help of the <u>Holy Spirit</u> within. Do the work; and let God handle the results. You cannot change anyone, but we can change ourselves and things begin to change around us.

NOTES

Part 2 of *Final*

Jesus tells the parable of the Loaned Money

> Jesus spoke in Matthew 25:14-29 "Again, it will be like a man going on a journey, who called his servants and entrusted his property to them. To one he gave five talents of money, to another two talents, and to another one talent, each according to his ability. Then he went on his journey. The man who had received the five talents went at once and put his money to work and gained five more. So also, the one with the two talents gained two more. But the man who had received the one talent went off, dug a hole in the ground and hid his master's money.
>
> "After a long time the master of those of those servants returned and settled accounts with them. The man who had received the five talents brought the other five, 'Master, he said you entrusted me with five talents. See, I have gained five more.'
>
> "His master replied, 'Well done, good and faithful servant! You have been faithful with a few things; I will put you in charge of many things. Come share your master's happiness!'
>
> "Then the man who had received the one talent came. 'Master', he said, 'I knew that you are a hard man, harvesting where you have not sown and gathering where you have not scattered seed. So I was afraid and went out and hid your talent in the ground. See here is what belongs to you.'
>
> "His master replied, 'You wicked, lazy servant! So you knew that I harvest where I have not sown and gather where I have not scattered seed? Well then, you should have put my money on deposit with the bankers, so that when I returned I would have received it back with interest.
>
> "Take the talent from him and give it to the one who has the ten talents. For everyone who has will be given more, and he will have an abundance. Whoever does not have, even what he has will be taken from him.'..." NIV

If you don't use your God given talents, you will lose them.
Where there is no risk,...there are no rewards!

NOTES

Part 3 Final

Noah Webster 1828…..cultivate

Cultivate

2. To improve by labor or study; to advance the growth of; to refine and improve by correction of faults, and enlargement of powers or good qualities; as, to cultivate talents; to cultivate a taste for poetry.

3. …to cultivate the mind.

3. To cherish; to foster; to labor to promote and increase; as to cultivate the love of excellence, to cultivate gracious affections.

Teach a man to fish or other skills, he will be independent with a foundation that will keep getting stronger. Keep giving him/her the fish and they will become more dependent, not able to build character strengths and foundation begins to weaken and crumble.

Digging deeper, those diamonds, the gems of "The Word of God" also reveals the treasure that is in each one of us. Cultivate!

I pray for all of God's people to be free from slavery (bondages), corruption, false gods, and to enjoy the freedoms which He has intended for all of His children.

NOTES

Bottom Line

✚ *Salvation here on earth and through eternity*
  ✚ *Faith in God and our Savior Jesus Christ*
    ✚ *Forgive others; as well as yourself*
✚ *Believe with an open heart=equals=liberation from mental and emotional bondage. One central key bondage I want to stress is the bondage of fears: fear of death, fear of old age, fear of poor health, disease, fear of over population, fear of over pollution to the environment, fear of no money, fear, fear, fear, can keep a person from seeing truths....a distortion in perception*
  ✚ *He provides life, insights, and*
    ✚ *ASK, pray, meditate on "His Word"*

Galatians 5:1, 4-5, 10, 13-18, 22-25

"It is for freedom that Christ has set us free. Stand firm, then and do not let yourselves be burdened again by a yoke of slavery. You who are trying to be justified by law have been alienated from Christ; you have fallen away from grace. But by faith, we eagerly await through the Spirit, the righteousness for which we hope. The one who is throwing you to confusion will pay the penalty.

You, my brothers were called to be free. But do not use your freedom to indulge the sinful nature; rather serve one another in love. The entire law is summed up in a single command: "Love your neighbor as yourself." If you keep on biting and devouring each other, watch out or you will be destroyed by each other.

So I say, live by the Spirit, you will not gratify the desires of the sinful nature. For the sinful nature desires what is contrary to the Spirit, you are not under law.

The acts of sinful nature are obvious ... (see NIV) I warn you, as I did before, that those who live like this will not inherit the kingdom of God.

But the fruit of the Spirit is love, joy, peace, patience, kindness, goodness, faithfulness, gentleness and self-control. Against such things there is no law."

NOTES

Part 2 *Bottom Line*

With Jesus in our hearts ♥ and the study of scripture, prayerfully, we begin to see things without a filter. That filter could be anger, guilt, and fear etc., unresolved emotions that we hold in our hearts ♥ which distorts our perception. That is why "Common Sense is Not so Common." These filters are blinding, keeping us in the dark, bondages that keep us from growing to full maturity, out of sync with God's love nature. With the "Spirit of Christ" in our hearts ♥, through a deep study of scripture, He releases one filter at a time.

"There is therefore no condemnation for those who are in Christ Jesus. For the law of the Spirit of life in Christ Jesus has set you free from the law of sin and of death." Romans 8:1-2

For the law of sin is immaturity; consequently, children leading instead of mature adults.

Sin nature is out of sync with God's nature.

N. Webster's 1828.....nature

NA´TURE

1. In *a general sense*, whatever is made or produced; a word that comprehends all the works of God; the universe. Of a phenix we say, there is no such thing in *nature*.

    And look through *nature* up to *nature's* God.   *Pope.*

2. By a metonymy of the **effect for the cause, nature is used for the agent, creator, author, producer of things**, or for the powers that produce them. By the expression, "trees and fossils are produced by *nature*," we mean, they are formed or produced by certain inherent powers in matter, or we mean that they are produced by God, the Creator, the Author of whatever is made or produced. The opinion that things are produced by inherent powers of matter, independent of a supreme intelligent author, is atheism. But generally men mean by *nature*, thus used, the Author of created things, or the operation of his power.

4. The established or regular course of things; as when we say, an event is **not according to nature**, or **it is out of the order of nature**.   *Boyle.*

5. A law or principle of action or motion in a natural body. A stone by *nature* falls, or inclines to fall.   *Boyle.*

Sin......out of order....out of sync with the nature of God! Blinding!

NOTES

Part 3 of Bottom Line

*Seek Him, nature's God, and make **Him #1** in your life* ♥

Hebrew 4:12-13 For the word of God is living and active. Sharper than any double-edged sword, it penetrates even to dividing soul and spirit, joints and marrow; it judges the thoughts and attitudes of the heart♥. Nothing in all creation is hidden from God's sight. Everything is uncovered and laid bare before the eyes of Him to whom we must give account. NIV

The God of truth, justice, love never to leave you nor forsake you. He is omniscient!

Walk in His nature, He is everywhere.

God of promises! Claim it!

For further study on promises of God:

"God of Promises" by Charles Stanley @ "In Touch Ministries" - http://www.intouch.org   CD, DVD or book.

Revelation 21:6-7…"It is done. I Am the Alpha and the Omega, the beginning and the end. I will give to the one who thirsts from the spring of the water of life without cost. He who overcomes shall inherit these things, and I will be his God." NASB

NOTES

Special Resources

"More Than A Carpenter" by Josh McDowell - *Still skeptical about Jesus....read this thin paperback of 120 pages and it will answer many of your questions.*

"The Montessori Method" by Maria Montessori *This book was first published in English 1912. The following description of this book was taken from the back cover.*

"Dr. Montessori (1870-1952), the first Italian woman M.D., was one of the great germinal pioneers in studying the intellectual development of the young child. Only through movement and manipulation, through thinking with the senses, does the child proceed to later "abstract thinking." Dr. Montessori carried her insight that children learned through all their senses, to its logical conclusion. On their way to "cleanliness, order, poise, and conversation," children use the Montessori materials-inherently logical and aesthetically pleasing-to develop a sense for order and logical thought, and a firm foundation for success in the three R's."

"The Montessori Revolution in Education" 1st edition 1962 by E.M.Standing (1887-1967)

Intro viii "Montessori's appeal was essentially to the spirit; and in this she was in contrast to many of the psychologists and pedagogues of her day. "A Teacher," she always maintained, "must not imagine that he can prepare himself for his vocation simply by acquiring knowledge and culture. Above all else he must cultivate within himself a proper attitude to the moral order."

Many people were eager to learn personally from Dr. Montessori

"Many of those did come; literally, from the ends of the earth to attend her famous international training courses, and was surprised at the effect this experience had upon them. They came simply expecting to hear lectures on child psychology the training of children, the teaching of various subjects, the management of children, and so forth. All these things they did receive in ample measure. But, as the months passed by they began to be aware that something else was happening too, something they had not expected; something different and more valuable, which they would have found difficult to put into words.

NOTES

They came with the intention of learning to help the child in his development and, to their surprise; they found that they were being unexpectedly helped in their own development. Subjects which they had disliked at school suddenly acquired a new and absorbing interest. New horizons were opening up before their minds, not only in the realm of the intellect but in the very meaning and scope of education. They experienced a genuine enlargement of mind and soul, and knew themselves, at the end of the course, to be different and greater than they were at the beginning. They realized that they had made a spiritual investment which would yield them interest as long as they lived-because life had taken on a new meaning and a richer promise."

http://www.christianmontessorifellowship.com

Principle Approach Method

http://www.face.net/?page=principle_approach

"The Principle Approach has been called "reflective teaching and learning." It is America's historic method of Biblical reasoning which places the Truths (or principles) of God's Word at the heart♥ of education. Each subject is predicated upon God's Biblical principles and students are taught to think and reason from principles and leading ideas using The Notebook Method to Research, Reason, Relate and Record."

I had learned the study of the Bible, utilizing the Concordance and Noah Webster's 1828 Dictionary from the Principle Approach method of teaching. I have used this method in my Bible studies for years and once I sit down to begin; it is very hard to stop. The lessons I receive are remarkable. This method teaches students from grades K to 12. The students will pull principles from the Bible in every subject. They have a notebook for each subject and they must write in their own words. At the end of the school year they have their own original works in each subject, and every year building blocks of growth. After attending a ten week course study, I felt cheated from my early and college education. Now, I am excited to learn and in subjects that I hated...I now love! And the teacher's enthusiasm is contagious, they love to teach and watch their students grow! Teachers also continually grow with the Principle Approach Method of Teaching.

NOTES

Works Cited (Books & CD-ROM)

Cloud, Henry, and John Townsend. BOUNDARIES, When to Say YES, When to Say NO, To Take Control of Your Life. Grand Rapids: Zondervan, 1992.

Fox, Emmet. The Sermon on the Mount: *The Key to Success in Life*. New York: HarperCollins, 1938.

Hebrew-Greek Key Word Study Bible - New American Standard Bible (NASB) Revised edition c. 1984, 1990, 2008 by AMG International, Inc. "Scripture taken from the NEW AMERICAN STANDARD BIBLE, 1960, 1962, 1963, 1968, 1971, 1972, 1973, 1975, 1977 by the Lockman foundation, Used by permission."

Life Application Bible – New International Version (NIV) Scripture quotations taken from the HOLY BIBLE, NEW INTERNATIONAL VERSION, Copyright 1973, 1978, 1984 by International Bible Society Used by permission of Zondervan Publishing House.

McDowell, Josh. More Than a Carpenter. Illinois: Tyndale House, 2005.

Montessori, Maria. The Montessori Method. New York: Schocken, 1964.

Slater, R. J. Teaching and Learning America's Christian History. San Francisco: Foundation for American Christian Education.

Standing, E. M. The Montessori Revolution in Education. New York: Schocken, 1970.

Webster, Noah. (1967 & 1995). American Dictionary of the English Language. Chesapeake, Virginia: Foundation for American Christian Education. (Original works published in 1828)

The Noah Webster 1828 Dictionary & King James Bible in Libronix CD-ROM March 3, 2008. Chesapeake, Virginia: Foundation for American Christian Education.

NOTES

Works Cited (Internet)

Anderson, Amy Rees. "Passive-Aggressive Behavior Will Destroy a Company's Culture." 06 March 2013. FORBES, Entrepreneurs. 23 September 2013. <http://www.forbes.com/sites/amyanderson/2013/03/06/passive-aggressive-behavior-will-destroy-a-companys-culture>.

Hartmann, Thom. "Thom Hartmann's Hunter and Farmer Approach to ADD/ADHD." 01 November 2007. THOM HARTMANN PROGRAM. News, Opinion, Debate. 23 September 2013. <http://www.thomhartmann.com/articles/2007/11/thom-hartmanns-hunter-and-farmer-approach-addadhd>.

Mayo clinic staff. "Being assertive: Reduce stress, communicate better. Assertiveness can help you control stress and anger and improve coping skills. Recognize and learn assertive behavior and communication." 17 June 2011. Mayo Clinic, Stress Management. 23 September 2013. <http://www.mayoclinic.com/health/assertive/SR00042>.

Simon, George. "Dealing with MANIPULATIVE people." 05 December 2010. Manipulative-people. 23 September 2013.< http://www.manipulative-people.com/aggressive-and-assertive-behavior>.

Simon, George. "Understanding the Aggressive Personalities." 11 March 2008. Counselling Resource, *Psychology, Philosophy & Real Life*. 23 September 2013. < http://counsellingresource.com/features/2008/11/03/aggressive-personalities>.

NOTES